Vocational Business

1

Business at Work

Keith Brumfitt, Stephen Barnes, Liz Norris & Jane Jones

Series Editor: Keith Brumfitt

Published in 2001 by:
Nelson Thornes Ltd
Delta Place
27 Bath Road
CHELTENHAM
GL53 7TH
United Kingdom

01 02 03 04 05 / 10 9 8 7 6 5 4 3 2 1

A catalogue record for this book is available from the British Library

ISBN 0 7487 6359 7

Illustrations by Oxford Designers and Illustrators

Page make-up and illustrations by GreenGate Publishing Services, Tonbridge, Kent

Printed and bound in Italy by Stige

1
Business at Work

Keith Brumfitt, Stephen Barnes, Liz Norris & Jane Jones

Contents

Introduction to Vocational Business series

This textbook is one of a series of six covering the core areas of business studies. Each book focuses on vocational aspects of business, rather than theoretical models, allowing the reader to understand how businesses operate. To complement this vocational focus, each book contains a range of case studies illustrating how businesses respond to internal and external changes.

The textbooks are designed to support students taking a range of business courses. While each is free standing, containing the essential knowledge required by the various syllabuses and course requirements, together they provide a comprehensive coverage of the issues facing both large and small businesses in today's competitive environment.

Titles in the series

Book 1   Business at Work
Book 2   The Competitive Business Environment
Book 3   Marketing
Book 4   Human Resources
Book 5   Finance
Book 6   Business Planning

Acknowledgements

The authors and publishers are grateful to the following organisations for permission to reproduce photographs and other material:
The Coca-Cola Company; The Co-operative Group; CRAC; The Dairy Council; Dancia international; East Kent Mercury; Horological Services, St Margaret's Bay; Ian Pearson/BT; Photodisc, Stockbyte, Foxx, Corel and Pictor.

Every effort has been made to contact copyright holders, and we apologise if any have been overlooked.

Business at Work

Introduction

This book explores business structures, cultures and organisation. It considers why some businesses are successful while others fail. Why do some close as quickly as they start up? Why are some dotcom businesses so successful while others have been spectacular flops? These are some of the questions you can explore in this book. In many ways it is both the starting point and the finishing point. We suggest you work through it first and return to it at the end of your course.

Figure 1.1 *All businesses, large and small, have objectives*

Why do businesses exist?

All businesses consist of individuals who work together to produce goods and services by combining the factors of production in such a way that they achieve their objectives.

Different business organisations have different objectives partly because they are run by different people for different reasons. These objectives could include:

- Making a profit (or surplus)
- Increasing sales
- Increasing market share
- Providing services to the community
- Charitable or non-profit making purposes
- Development of a skilled workforce
- Achieving employee satisfaction and/or security
- Providing or improving customer satisfaction
- Offering high quality goods or services
- Improving and/or maintaining efficiency
- Survival as a business
- Caring for the environment.

Most organisations have several objectives. Businesses have to decide which objectives are the most important at any one time and make decisions based on this. Obviously, as businesses and the world around them change, their objectives change. A business which has just been set up may want to focus initially on building up a good market share and therefore keep its prices low. As it becomes more established it may decide to concentrate more on its profitability. Consequently it might increase prices and seek to develop better customer services. Eventually, as profits rise it may feel that it can focus on broader objectives.

CASE STUDY

Mid-Kent Water

Caring for the environment

Mid-Kent Water has a duty to the company's shareholders to make sufficient profits to provide them with a decent return on their investment. At the same time, it is expected to provide a wide variety of services to the community for supplying water and processing sewage. Like many organisations it is also judged on the extent to which it is active on environmental issues. These objectives may conflict. Money invested in new reservoirs may improve the service to customers but could reduce the profitability of the company and may, where new construction is required, have a negative effect upon the environment.

Shareholders, page 7

CASE STUDY

Public sector v private sector

Does the public sector really have different objectives to the private sector?

There has been criticism of the changing priorities in public sector activities such as health care and education. Public services are increasingly held accountable for the money they spend. Managers are often thought to spend more time and effort on managing the finances than on the more traditional 'soft' objectives such as providing a service to the community. A recent study showed that most managers in the public sector see their objectives differently to managers in the private sector.

Table 1.1 Managers' most important goals by sector

Goal	Public	Private	Voluntary
Provide or improve customer satisfaction and/or service to the community	31%	7%	20%
Improve and/or maintain efficiency	16%	9%	12%
Make a difference personally	11%	10%	11%
Achieve employee satisfaction and/or security	10%	3%	2%

Source: Public Management Foundation. Weighted Values: Harnessing the Commitment of Managers

Key terms

Private sector – organisations owned and controlled by individuals.
Public sector – organisations owned and/or controlled by the government.
Voluntary sector – charitable organisations which operate as independent bodies.

Types of business organisation

There are many ways of categorising different organisations: according to size, location, type of product, etc. One of the most useful ways is according to who owns the organisation. In the UK, all organisations fall into one of three main categories:
- the private sector
- the public sector
- the voluntary sector

Key terms

Establishment – individual factory, plant or office.
Business – firm which is considered to be a single unit though it may operate from several different establishments.
Enterprise – one or more businesses under common ownership.
Parent company – often called a holding company. It often exists only to hold shares in other companies that offer products or services.
Subsidiary companies – companies owned by other companies.

3

Who owns what?

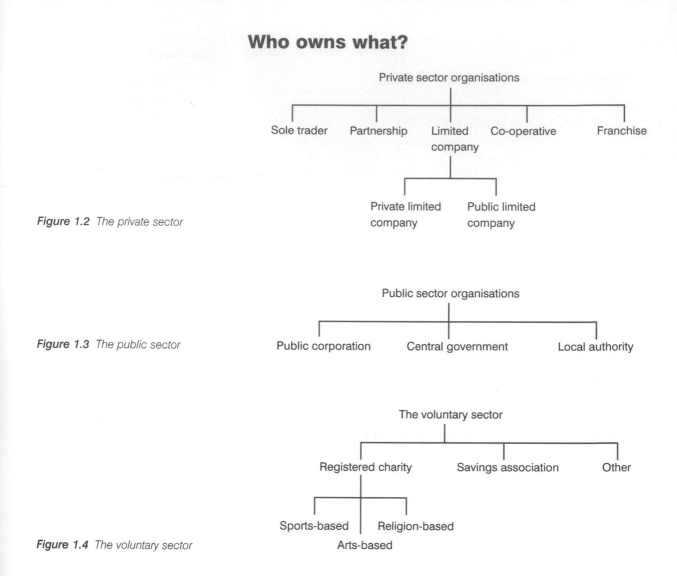

Figure 1.2 *The private sector*

Figure 1.3 *The public sector*

Figure 1.4 *The voluntary sector*

❘ Which organisation is best?

Would you go it alone?

In any locality there are lots of examples of sole traders: window cleaners, hairdressers, newsagents, taxi drivers and plumbers are often sole traders. We spoke to Rajinder Basi who came to the UK from Uganda where he had his own business. He decided to set up a taxi company in the UK.

Figure 1.5 Starting again

ⓒASE STUDY

Rajinder Basi

Taxi for hire

'One of the problems with being a sole trader is that if the business fails I will lose everything. My solicitor calls this unlimited liability, which means that I would have to sell my house, my cars and my furniture. If this isn't sufficient to pay off the business's debts I might be taken to court and declared bankrupt. About the only things I would be able to keep are the beds we sleep on and the clothes we stand up in! The thing is, though, that while we are relatively small the tax position is better for us.

It wasn't easy finding enough money to set up the business. I brought some money with me from Uganda and borrowed money from my brother-in-law, my father-in-law and my brother to buy a car and set up an office in Chatham. My bank manager was very helpful when I needed a bank loan to buy a second taxi recently. He has also been quite good with overdrafts, particularly when I had just started and was building up a pool of regular customers.

It was particularly difficult finding my way through all the different types of loans available and their cost. Rates of interest paid for borrowing varied from base rate plus 0.75% to base rate plus 4%. However, differences in the way the annual percentage rate (APR) is calculated made direct comparisons difficult. Similarly I had to compare things such as:
* how long I could borrow the money for
* whether I could just pay interest for the first few months rather than making capital repayments as well

Key term

Base rate – this is the rate of interest set each month by the Bank of England Monetary Policy Committee. It is used by all banks and other financial institutions as a base for their rates. Savings rates tend to be below base and lending rates above.

5

- whether I could meet the loan repayments if business wasn't as good as I had projected
- penalties for early repayment.

I could go on and on. It took several weeks to explore the possibilities, make comparisons, bargain with lenders and eventually settle on a deal.

I'm basically self-employed and I enjoy being my own boss. I have complete control over who I employ, the decisions I take and, of course, I get to keep all the profits. The downside is that it is difficult to borrow money from banks. If I'm off sick I earn nothing at all and I frequently work from seven in the morning until nine at night without a break. I've also had to learn basic book-keeping skills, customer service and, of course, when I first came to this country I had to pass my driving test and apply for a special licence from Rochester on Medway District Council before I could even begin trading.'

When we spoke to other sole traders in different businesses their experiences were very similar to Rajinder's. Some said that other advantages include the fact that they provide a personal service that encourages customers to come back over and over again. On the other hand, many felt annoyed by how difficult it was to get discounts from their suppliers because they did not buy large enough quantities at any one time. Some also said that the banks were not as helpful as their advertising literature suggests.

ACTIVITY

Organise a small survey of three local sole traders. What were their experiences of setting up in business?

Key term

Partnership – a group of two or more individuals working together in a business with a view to making a profit.

Two's company?

Partnerships are usually set up where there is a need for extra money, new skills or ideas, more customer contacts or help with running the business. There are few legal formalities for setting up a partnership and they are popular with the professions. There must be at least two people and a maximum of 20, though the 1985 Companies Act allows accountants, solicitors and members of any recognised stock exchange to have more than 20 partners. Normally partners have unlimited liability, which means that each partner could be made to pay all the debts of the partnership. For this reason, it is advisable to make sure that the people with whom you form a partnership are reliable.

There is a form of limited partnership although it is not found very frequently. With this, at least one partner, known as a sleeping partner, takes no active role in the day-to-day running of the business but simply contributes capital in return for a share of the profits. Partnerships are common with shops, doctors, vets, insurance brokers, builders and small manufacturing businesses.

If you look in the Yellow Pages you will find lots of examples of small accounting firms. We interviewed Sarah Chapman who is a partner in Morris Chapman Chartered Accountants.

Ⓒ ASE STUDY

Sarah Chapman

Choosing a partner

'When my children were small, I used to work from home doing the books for small businesses and providing tax advice to individuals and companies. More and more people wanted advice, particularly with self-assessment, so at the beginning of this year I decided to go into partnership.

I advertised in the *Liverpool Echo* and interviewed several people. Bill Morris was the obvious choice because he had money to invest, which meant that we could rent office space in town and he specialises in audit which is a new service I can offer to my existing customers besides attracting new ones. Having a partner has reduced some of the burden of decision-making. It also means that I can now take holidays without feeling guilty or letting customers down. When the children are ill I can always take a day off.

I suppose the disadvantage of working with someone else is that there may come a time when we have a major disagreement. That's one of the reasons why we decided to have a Deed of Partnership. Although we don't see any reason why we should stop working as a partnership in the near future we have had to consider what will happen if one of us dies, is declared bankrupt or wants to leave. As the law stands, the partnership will automatically end if one of these things happens.

Unlimited liability means that each of us is personally responsible for all of the business's debts but that's no different from being a sole trader. We share the profits equally but provided we attract the extra business this shouldn't reduce my income, although while we are building the partnership I may be a bit worse off than I would have been as a sole trader.'

Figure 1.6 *Sarah Chapman and her partner were able to rent office space in town*

Key terms

Limited liability – if the business fails, the owners (shareholders) will only lose the money they have put into the business and will not have to repay the business's debts.
Shareholders – the owners of a company.
Private limited company – the use of the letters 'Ltd' or 'Limited' after the company name shows that the company is a private limited company (e.g. Littlewoods Ltd).
Companies Registration Office (Companies House) – the government body responsible for maintaining records on UK-based limited companies.

Going limited

A limited company is a legal body which is distinct from the shareholders who own the company. Companies operate under their own name and have their own rights and responsibilities. Companies are run

Stock exchange, page 9

by Boards of Directors who are not necessarily shareholders. Most private limited companies have a relatively small number of shareholders who each own a large 'share' of the company. Very often the shareholders or their families also run the business. Individual shareholders in private limited companies often have control over what the company does because they own large percentages of the company. Shares cannot be bought or sold on the Stock Exchange.

With public limited companies there are usually hundreds, thousands or even millions of shareholders, most of whom own a very small stake in the company and have little or no contact with it on a day-to-day basis. Generally these shareholders have little control or influence over what the company does, and they own the shares as an investment. The only shareholders who tend to have large enough stakes to be able to control public limited companies are pension funds and life assurance companies.

Limited companies must have their accounts audited each year by independent accountants. The accounts must be filed with the Companies Registration Office which allows members of the public to obtain a copy. In addition they have to hold an annual general meeting of the shareholders each year.

You'll find many examples of private limited companies since about half a million businesses are set up like this. We visited Continental Britannia Line Limited, who ship scrap metal into and out of the UK. The fourteen shareholders who are mostly family and friends have each contributed between £1,000 and £10,000 to buy shares in the company. One of the directors spoke to us about his experience.

CASE STUDY

Continental Britannia Line Limited

Cruel Britannia

'When we set up the business we decided to become a private limited company straight away because it gave us more credibility with the large international companies who were our customers. While it helped with our customers it created a bit of a problem with our suppliers since the word 'Limited' after our name warned them that if we did run up business debts that the company couldn't pay they wouldn't be able to claim the money from the shareholders.

We also thought that having limited liability would protect the shareholders from some of the risks of the business. It was essential in overcoming the reluctance of people to buy shares. Having said that, we all had to provide personal guarantees to the bank so that if the company failed to meets its repayments on the bank loan, we would personally be liable to repay it. This somewhat reduces the value of limited liability.

One of the advantages of being a limited company is that the money that shareholders have invested in the business does not have to be repaid to them. If someone wishes to stop being a shareholder they can only do that if they find somebody else who wants to buy their shares. The company itself is not involved and it just continues to run regardless of who its shareholders are. When we started up we thought we'd be able to run the company by ourselves. What we didn't realise is that in addition to knowing about shipping we needed to be able to do all the administration and accounting that went with it. As a limited company it was easy to appoint a third director with this expertise.'

Going public

Approximately 3 per cent of companies are public limited companies and many started as private limited companies, like Lucas Varity plc. As they grew and required more capital they decided to 'go public' and float their shares, usually on the Stock Exchange or the Unlisted Securities Market. They have to conform with all the legal requirements of a private limited company but because their shares are available to the public there are stricter rules about how they govern themselves and what information they provide about themselves.

Companies decide to go public because it is easier to obtain finance, both through issuing new shares and borrowing from banks. However, going public is expensive and there are ongoing legal and financial requirements. Some public limited companies find that as they grow larger they lose control over many aspects of the business's operations. The major shareholders of many public limited companies are investment institutions such as the Prudential Insurance Company and Scottish Life.

Key terms

Public limited company – any company whose shares can be owned by the general public.
Multinational corporation – an increasing number of businesses are owned by companies which operate on a worldwide basis, e.g. Ford Motor Company, the Sony Corporation, Nestlé.
Stock Exchange – the main market within the UK for buying and selling shares.
Unlisted Securities Market – new or small companies often decide to float (launch) their shares on this market before progressing to the International Stock Exchange.

CASE STUDY

Lucas Varity plc

Going for broke

Lucas Varity is one of the world's leading car brake specialists. The company was created when Britain's leading components maker, Lucas Industries and US engineer, Varity Corporation, merged in 1996. Its stated aim is to 'hold leading positions in attractive growth markets'. The letters 'plc' after a company's name indicate that it is a public limited company.

Facts

What is it worth?	£3.88 billion
How many people does it employ?	57,000

Is ownership important?

Many consultants and business analysts argue that it is the product that matters rather than who owns a business. But shoppers and other buyers care more than you might think. Angry consumers have, in the past, inflicted major boycotts on the products of Barclays Bank, Shell and Nestlé when they did not like the companies' policies even though such policies did not in any way affect the products that they were buying.

 Parent company, page 3

However, while all products must by law carry an address you can write to, there is no need to put the address of the parent company on the product. If you buy a product made by a household name such as Kraft, Jacobs or Suchard you have no way of knowing that these companies are owned by the tobacco giant Philip Morris. There is even less chance of knowing that the Chinese government owns part of HSBC (Hong Kong and Shanghai Banking Corporation) which owns Midland Bank.

Ownership matters

ⒸASE STUDY

Virgin Group

Ownership matters

Ownership is particularly important to Richard Branson who, in 1986, decided to float a substantial part of his Virgin Group as a public limited company in order to raise more capital for expansion. A large drop in the price of Virgin shares put a stop to this plan. Two years later he decided to buy back the shares and return Virgin to being a private limited company.

One of the reasons for this was that Branson was unhappy with the way in which the large financial and investment institutions tried to influence the way he ran the business. These institutions wanted to make profits quickly for their investors whereas he was more concerned with the long-term future of the business.

Co-operation – does it work?

The first co-operative was formed in 1844 when a group of low-paid workers got together to buy goods and groceries in bulk at a discount. Co-operatives grew in popularity and at their peak in the 1950s there were a thousand separate societies. In 1983 there were 9 million co-op members and 7,000 shops. Since then their market share has declined as a result of growing competition from the supermarket chains.

Key terms

Co-operative – this is a special type of legal entity which is set up for the mutual benefit of a group of people. These may be the people working in the business (a worker co-operative), the people who buy the products of the business (a consumer/retail co-operative), or a group of small businesses who get together for marketing purposes (a marketing co-operative).

Mutuals – set up by members for their own benefit. Four categories are recognised by law: building societies, friendly societies, credit unions and catch-all 'industrial and provident societies'.

Building societies – use savers' deposits to lend to house buyers.

Friendly societies – group of regulated, relatively small businesses offering insurance and enjoying tax exemptions.

Credit unions – small-scale banks run by volunteers or people with a social mission.

Industrial and provident societies – these include trade unions, housing associations and various clubs and co-operatives.

Figure 1.7 (Reproduced by permission of The Co-operative Group)

The Co-op continues to be owned by members of the society. Anyone can become a member by buying a share for £1. A Board of Directors runs the business. This is elected by individual members who each have one vote regardless of the number of shares they hold.

CASE STUDY

The Co-op

Running to catch up

The Co-operative Wholesale Society (CWS) is probably best known for its retail stores but it is also Britain's largest farming business, the largest organiser of funerals and the owner of a very successful bank and insurance company.

The Co-op has been a study in decline. Six years ago CWS retail sales were £1.5 billion. At a time of huge growth for other retailers, CWS sales increased by only 4.2 per cent in 1997 and profits remained static. In comparison, Tesco sales doubled and Somerfield's profits trebled to £115 million, although they did not experience the same growth in sales.

The reward/loyalty cards which have been so successful for Tesco and Sainsbury are not a new concept. For years shoppers at the Co-op were paid 15 per cent of their bills in a twice yearly dividend. However, this has now stopped because profits have declined so drastically.

Why hasn't the Co-op been able to mirror the success of the other major retailers?

- Failure to introduce scanning checkout technology promptly, let alone computers able to calculate the dividends
- Much lower margins than competitors
- Investments not enough to catch up with the market leaders.

The Co-op has recently reworked its business strategy and concluded that taking competitors on head to head is a loser. They will concentrate on two core markets:

- small convenience stores in town centres
- supermarkets in towns with no superstore nearby.

The focus is on refurbishing smaller stores to make them less like mini supermarkets and more like a corner shop – somewhere to get a newspaper, fresh bread or something you forgot at the supermarket. The Co-op believes that secondary shopping (as opposed to the main visits made to shops) is growing very rapidly. It accounts for 30–40 per cent of total food shopping. They would rather be the brand leader in the top-up market than second in the main shopping market.

CWS is also now exploiting links with the Co-operative Retail Society, the movement's other big retailer, the Co-operative Bank and

Key term

Dividend – a sum of money paid regularly to its shareholders out of its profits.

the CIS (Co-operative Insurance Society). The possibilities are good but Tesco and Sainsbury have already beaten them to it with financial services available through their supermarkets. Again, it is a case of too little too late.

Other mutuals

There is no clear distinction between a not-for-profit company, a mutual, a voluntary organisation and a charity. There is a range of overlapping legal definitions and regulatory bodies. At best they offer the comfort of 'self administration'. If you add the voluntary sector (estimated to turn over £20 billion a year) to the mutuals, probably some 350,000 separate organistions fall into this category. This is a sizable section of the UK's economy not working for profit.

An important sub-section of this category is the group of building societies and insurance organisations which developed in the nineteenth century. Members' savings were recycled as loans to homebuyers to enable people to buy their own home. In recent years their success has allowed them to accumulate large surpluses. As a result many, led by Abbey National in the 1980s, have converted to plc status. Members were offered windfall share allocations which could be sold to raise cash or kept as invesments. The conversion of Abbey National has been followed by the Woolwich, Halifax, and Bradford and Bingley. Similarly pension and insurance companies such as Sun Life of Canada and Scottish Widows have now given up their mutual status.

However, about 70 societies have remained as mutuals with £140 billion of assets and 15 million investors. They compete actively against the new plcs by narrowing the gap between interest rates offered to savers and the rates received for mortgages. As Michael Burnstein of Morgan Stanley Dean Witter in New York says: 'I suspect the same forces are at work the world over. How do mutuals compete with diversified stockholder-owned companies? They don't have the capital, they don't have the economies of scale and they don't have the currency to motivate management and employees.' Even so, members of some mutuals have resisted very attractive offers to be bought out by larger companies or to go public. They claim they like the independence and personal service offered by the mutuals.

Non-profit-making organisations

These are organisations which frequently use business methods but do not intend to make profits for their owners. These include registered charities. These are legally established organisations which are listed in the Central Register of Charities. They are controlled by the Charity Commissioners, who ensure that they are properly set up to raise money for educational, religious, community or relief of poverty causes. They benefit from special tax advantages.

> ### Key term
> **Economies of scale** – savings which occur as a result of the size of the organisation.

13

They may be organised on an international basis like the Red Cross; a national basis such as the RSPCA (Royal Society for the Prevention of Cruelty to Animals) or locally, for example the Demelza House Hospice for Children in Kent. They may also be used to raise money through one-off events like Red Nose Day.

They frequently have large budgets for advertising, marketing and fund-raising activities and they are occasionally criticised for spending too little on their cause and too much on administration.

Franchising – the best of both worlds?

If you look in the business advertisements section of your local newspaper you will see a number of offers of franchises from all sorts of businesses. There is also a specialist publication called *Business Franchise Magazine* which will give you some idea of the cost of buying franchises, and the training, equipment, materials, marketing and help in finding premises that franchisees can expect. This can vary enormously depending on the reputation of the franchisor and the business potential in your local area.

Your local milkman is probably a franchisee. Bill McLachlan, who is our milkman, is franchised with Unigate Dairies. Two years ago the dairy offered him the chance to franchise his round for £5,000. We asked him why he decided to take them up on their offer given that he was already employed by them as a milkman.

Figure 1.8 Going it alone, but with support. (Reproduced by permission of The Dairy Council.)

ⒸASE STUDY

Unigate Dairies

Going it alone but with support

'It was not easy deciding to take up the offer since it meant that I had to raise £5,000. My first reaction to this was who on earth was going to lend me £2,000 which is what I was short of since I had £3,000 in savings. In fact, when I went to the bank they were very willing to lend me the money as I would be linked to a well known franchisor – Unigate. As far as they are concerned there is much less chance of a small business failing when it franchises from such a company.

The main attraction was that I would be more of my own boss. Now, I have a vested interest in getting new customers as well as keeping my old ones since I share in the profits. I feel I have something to strive for.

The nice thing about a franchise is that although I'm my own boss, Unigate provides me with a lot of support in marketing and promotion. For example, I don't have to worry about special offer leaflets as these are provided by them. It does involve some uncertainties. For instance,

I have to buy all my supplies from them, not just milk but potatoes, meat and seasonal goods. Normally that's fine because I get these cheaper than I could buy them at the local cash and carry because Unigate are able to buy in bulk. Now and again, I get a chance to buy something very cheaply from a local farmer but my agreement with Unigate won't let me. I suppose I'm not entirely my own boss but it's a small price to pay for all the support I receive.'

From a franchisor's point of view the main advantage of a franchise is that it can help the business to grow quickly without the owners having to raise all the capital directly. A chain of businesses can be quickly established without huge investment. In addition to saving capital costs, franchisors save on day-to-day operating costs such as wages, materials and administration. Since they are self-employed, franchisees are highly motivated and committed. As a result there is a smaller risk of failure for a franchised business than for a similar business which does not operate as a franchise. By sharing, franchisors can expand while franchisees benefit from buying into an already successful business. But, like any business, nothing is certain although survival among franchises is higher than among businesses set up independently.

CASE STUDY

Dancia International

Tutus, tights and tap shoes

Figure 1.9

Dancing is a multi-million pound growth industry. The market for specialist shoes for salsa, tap, flamenco and other crazes is thriving. One company, Dancia International, based in Brighton, is Britain's first specialist dancewear franchise. They retail footwear from rock'n'roll boots to tap shoes, and clothes from tutus to tights and cowboy shirts to leotards. To set up a franchise with Dancia International you need £13,000 in cash in order to pay for the franchise fee, stock, full training and shop fittings. The shop, unlike most retail businesses, does not have to be in a prime city centre location – just near or close to reasonable parking. The company's owner, Diane Kirkup, and husband, Tim, say you can expect to have a turnover of £125,000 in three years' time. Profits will then be around £30,000–£40,000.

Table 1.2 *What form of business organisation is best?*

	Sole trader	Partner-ship	Private Limited Company (Ltd)	Public Limited Company (plc)	Co-operative	Franchise
Legally easy to set up	Yes	Yes	No	No	No	No
Easy to raise finance	No	No	Yes	Yes	Yes	Yes
Separation of ownership and control	No	No	Yes	Yes	Yes	No
Limited liability	No	No	Yes	Yes	Yes	No
Job specialisation possible	No	Yes	Yes	Yes	Yes	No
Separate legal identity	No	No	Yes	Yes	Yes	No
Share capital	No	No	Yes	Yes	Yes	No
Shares available to public	No	No	No	Yes	No	No
Profits not shared	Yes	No	No	No	No	No
Accounts not published	Yes	Yes	No	No	No	Yes
Quick decision-making	Yes	Yes	No	No	No	Yes
Low risk of business failure	No	No	No	Yes	Yes	Yes

Key terms

Public corporations are separate legal organisations which have been established by Acts of Parliament. Privatisation occurs when public sector assets are sold to the private sector, e.g. gas, coal, telecommunications.

IPOC – Independent Publicly Owned Corporation. These have charters setting out their objectives (such as delivery of the service to every home or office). Their prices will be agreed with a regulator who ensures universal service is ring-fenced and not subsidised by other operations. The government holds share capital and receives dividends. The Board of Directors is independent from the government for all operational decisions including major investments. They are also allowed to borrow on the capital markets.

| Public sector organisations

Throughout the twentieth century the role of the state grew as governments sought to manage the economy more effectively. As a result the UK government bought many industries and produced a large number of goods and services itself, such as defence, police and the judiciary, local government and street lighting.

There are many different types of public ownership in the UK.

- Public corporations, e.g. the BBC, the Bank of England. The boards are appointed by a government minister and they are free to manage their own affairs on a day-to-day basis although the government can give general directions on policy issues. Many, such as the Post Office, want to become Independent Publicly Owned Corporations (IPOC).
- Companies, where the government has a majority shareholding. These operate under the same conditions as other private and public limited companies.
- Enterprises that are part of government departments, such as the Inland Revenue which is part of the Treasury.
- Executive Agencies that are public services, such as the Central Statistical Office, the Royal Mint, Companies House and the Child Benefits Agency. These are separate from the related government department to enable them to function in a more cost-effective way. They control their own budgets.
- Quangos (quasi-autonomous non-government organisations) or non-departmental government bodies (NDPB) generally control

large budgets with limited accountability to the government. This gives them their name 'quasi-autonomous', which means that they are semi-independent. The number of these has grown significantly in recent years. Many activities will bring you into contact with an organisation run by a quango. For example, your local hospital will be run by the local hospital trust and if you are on Training Credits, a Modern Apprenticeship or New Deal you will have come into contact with your local Learning and Skills Council.

- Business activities run by local authorities, including swimming pools, leisure centres, golf courses, car parks, waste collection and payroll. Many of these are not run directly by local authorities. Although the authorities are responsible for ensuring the provision and quality of such services they are subject to compulsory competitive tendering. Private sector organisations bid to provide these services and are frequently successful. For example, in some local authorities school dinners are provided by a subsidiary of Rentokil plc.

The nature of the relationship between the government and its businesses is not the same as it used to be. Throughout the 1980s and 1990s many industries were privatised. The reasons for this are various but generally include:

- reduction of government involvement in industry
- improvements in efficiency in both the privatised companies, e.g. British Airways, and the remaining public sector
- reduction in the Public Sector Borrowing Requirement (both through the proceeds of the sale and a reduction in the need to invest)
- weakening of the power of trade unions in public sector wage bargaining
- widening of share ownership among the public
- encouraging share ownership by employees.

There are many household names which used to be public sector organisations. These were sold to the general public through share offerings, for example, British Aerospace, British Airports Authority, British Airways, British Gas, British Steel, Cable and Wireless, Jaguar Cars, Rolls Royce, and the regional water companies. Other public sector businesses were sold to private companies.

Some of the public utilities, e.g. gas, electricity, water, have their prices and other policies regulated by government-appointed agencies.

Table 1.3 Regulatory agencies

OFTEL	Office of Telecommunications. This body is being merged in 2001 with the Independent Television Commission (ITC), the Radio Authority and the Broadcasting Standards Authority to form OFCOM which will cover all public service broadcasting
OFWAT	Office of Water Services
OFFER	Office of Electricity Regulation
OFGAS	Office of Gas Supply

Central government in the UK is formed by the political party with the largest number of MPs in the House of Commons. The Head of State (the Queen) asks the leader of this party to form a government. The Prime Minister is the leader of this government and ministers head the various sections of the government, such as the Ministry of Defence and the Department for Education and Employment. These departments are run by permanent staff who are known as civil servants. Ministers usually deal with policies while civil servants carry out the policy decided by the government. However, civil servants do advise ministers on policy issues.

Local government in the UK is run by local councils whose members are elected to run a wide range of services for the local community such as education, social services, street lighting and refuse collection. As with central government, the elected representatives (councillors) are usually responsible for policy, and local government employees carry out these policies. However, their ability to decide policy is limited by the requirements of central government and legislation.

The government has increasingly subjected public sector activities (local and national) to competitive pressures through a variety of means. These include competitive tendering where services such as cleaning, gardening, computer services and refuse collection are bought in from private companies by the public sector organisations. The health service, the civil service, local authority schools and others have to employ the business which offers the best price regardless of whether it is a department of their own organisation or a private company.

Dividends, page 12

The Public Sector Borrowing Requirement (PSBR) shows the amount the government needs to borrow each year in order to finance the difference between its spending and its income (i.e. its deficit). If the government repays previous loans there is a Public Sector Debt Repayment (PSDR), such as happened in the March 2001 budget.

This is what we call a SWOT analysis.

CASE STUDY

The Post Office

The third way between privatisation and state ownership

The Post Office became a public corporation in 1969, reporting to the Ministry for Trade and Industry. Its businesses consist of the Royal Mail, Parcelforce, Post Office Counters and subscription services such as issuing Road Fund licences and TV licences.

For some years governments have reviewed Post Office operations and proposed both partial and full privatisation but the proposals have been dropped in the face of public opposition. The Post Office is able to expand its businesses and this is the main argument for not radically altering its structure. Full privatisation is not thought to be an option but a partial privatisation which brings in private sector funds may provide the Treasury with a lump sum and a regular income from the dividends.

The future is not clear. The Post Office has some strong growth markets such as leafleting and advertising but the growth of the Internet and e-mail is beginning to herald a profound change in the way we communicate.

Table 1.4 *What does the future hold for the Post Office?*

Strengths	Weaknesses
• Next day delivery to the doorstep • Good profitability • Competitive prices	• Public corporation status • Lack of commercial freedom • Subject to public sector pay policy • Profit restraints – if profits are greater than an agreed level they are paid to the Treasury • Unable to diversify fully
Opportunities	Threats
• Growing share of the call centre market • Potential for takeovers, joint ventures and long-term deals • Possibility of becoming an IPOC • Delivery of e-commerce products	• Very competitive market • Growing liberalisation of European and world postal markets • Use of fax, e-mail and the Internet

Ⓐ CTIVITY

How will the business activities of e-commerce companies such as lastminute.com and amazon.com affect the Post Office?

Ⓐ CTIVITY

Is this the end as we know it?

The Post Office is planning a £3 billion assault on the European postal market, aiming to build a major position In every EU country by the year 2008. Given the greater commercial freedom, how can it do this?

The EU plans to reduce state monopolies on the delivery of letters in 2002 with the possibility of all restrictions going in 2008. What problems will this create for the Post Office? Who do you think will be its main competitors? Have you mainly thought of British companies? Are there large players in the European market?

In 1999 the Post Office paid £300 million for a stake in German Parcel as well as £10 million for Williams, an Irish postal company. It has also bought into City Post, a firm in the US bulk delivery market. This has given it a 3 per cent share of the European market. How can this be increased in the next eight years or so?

The government has affected Post Office business by announcing its intentions to switch the payment of state benefits, such as pensions, to banks by 2003. This accounts for 30 to 35 per cent of some sub-post offices' work and £400 million of revenue.

Plans to close several hundred urban post offices have been put on hold as a result of continuing negotiations on the setting up of a post office based bank – The Universal Bank – funded partly by the major high street banks. This will provide basic bank accounts for the financially excluded and it could restore £150 million of the £400 million yearly revenue which post offices will lose when benefits are paid directly into bank accounts. Attempts to create the new bank have been opposed by the major banks although they recognise that the government may decide to fund it by introducing a windfall tax if negotiations break down. While the government is encouraging small post offices to merge, many businesses are not willing to take the plunge unless they can be sure they will be getting Universal Bank revenue and, of course, compensation packages for mergers.

1 How many sub-post offices are there in your town or the area you live in? Which ones could merge?
2 Conduct a survey to find out their main functions. Don't forget that many fulfil social functions as well. What might those be? What other services could they provide particularly if a couple of smaller offices and their associated shops were merged to form a larger unit?

Village post office in 'use it or lose it' plea

The end of the village post office would be the downfall of Kingsdown's small community, forcing people to shop in the nearest town.

This is the belief of Celia Cotton, who owns the post office which has been in the village since 1930.

Now she is keeping her fingers crossed about the uncertain future of her business, following changes which mean people can draw pensions from banks as well as post offices.

Mrs Cotton told the Mercury: "Pensions are our main bread and butter at the moment, but soon they will be payable anywhere."

"So I think some of us will close so the rest of us can survive."

Pressure

But Mrs Cotton has distributed leaflets throughout the village outlining new services her post office offers and promoting the motto 'use it or lose it.' It points out the post office is not immune from commercial pressure.

Customers of Alliance and Leicester, Barclays, Cahoot, The Co-operative Bank, Lloyds TSB and National Savings can withdraw and deposit money from Kinsdown post office as part of the changes.

Mrs Cotton said: "The future of Kingsdown post office is uncertain. If it closed it would affect the other shops in the village.

The business is run by Mrs Cotton with four part-time staff. As well as a post office service, the shop sells confectionery, greetings cards and stationery.

It has a loyal customer base, who believe the business is essential to the village community.

Jan Narborough, who lives in Church Cliff, uses the post office regularly and said it was a vital service.

"I collect my child benefit, pick up a lot of stamps for my business and do a lot of posting here rather than take things to town.

I only wish I could do my car tax here. But I have to go to Deal for that," she added.

A Post Office spokesman said: "We are keen to maintain our network and have no intention of closing any of our post offices.

"Every year we derive fees for handling business on behalf of the Government but that money will go out of the window.

"We are looking at ways we can make up the shortfall, including universal banking. We are also installing computers at all our branches."

3 Record your findings on a spread sheet and produce bar charts, pie charts and other suitable diagrams to illustrate.

4 What will be the main effects of switching benefits payments to banks in your area? What are the main forms of benefits paid at Post Offices? Given that if you receive benefits you can currently have them paid into your bank account why don't the majority of people choose this method?

5 How far have negotiations got for a Universal Bank partly funded by the major banks? Why are the banks dragging their feet? What have they got to lose if they don't go along with the Universal Bank plan?

Postal Services Act

New legislation in the Postal Services Act will convert the Post Office into a plc. The Act will also allow the Post Office to borrow at commercial rates as well as reduce the amount of profit it gives to the government from 80 per cent to 40 per cent. Just prior to the conversion Post Office profits fell by £56 million to £608 million. In that period it paid £310 million to the Treasury. What effect will these changes have on

1 government income?

2 investment by the Post Office?

The sub-post office in your area is closing and the local community is starting a campaign to save it. As you've done so much research and have collected so much information you are asked to help.

Tasks

1 Draw up a small advertisement detailing the meeting which is being organised.

2 Write a short article for your local paper outlining the purpose of the meeting and the place and time.

3 What is the new name of the Post Office Group? Check in newspapers of January 2001.

Figure 1.10 Use it or lose it. (East Kent Mercury, 15 March 2001.)

4 Divide your group into sub-groups. One should present the Post Office case to the meeting and the other the case of the local community. It would be fun to enact this as a role play with some good old-fashioned heckling from the 'local community' group. Perhaps you could get a local business to sponsor you in this venture and judge the results, with the donation of a small 'prize' for the group which 'wins' the day. Even if it's just a burger, chips and free cola at a local restaurant it would be worth it and you might even get some free publicity for your school or college!

How organisations operate

Why do they exist? Mission and objectives

Decision making lies at the heart of management. Decisions have to be made about what to produce, how to produce it, at what price, when and where. This involves many secondary decisions, some of which are fundamental and others of which are routine everyday tasks.

In order to make clear rational decisions, organisations need to have a good idea of what they are trying to achieve and how best to achieve it. This entails identifying their objectives, outlining the problems, collecting the data, recognising the alternative courses of action, evaluating the choices and implementing the decisions.

Why have objectives?

Organisations need to define their objectives and put in place a management structure that enables sound business decisions to be made and carried out.

Table 1.5 *Mission*

Objectives	Management Responsibility	Timeframe
Strategic objectives or the overall plans of the organisation, e.g. major capital investment, new products, etc.	Directors/ senior management	Long-term
Tactical objectives concerning the use of resources to achieve the organisational goals, e.g. minor capital investments, changes to marketing activities, etc.	Divisional managers	Medium-term
Operational objectives concerning stock levels, planning schedules, credit control, etc.	Departmental managers	Short-term

Key terms

....

Mission statement – a very general statement about what the organisation is seeking to do or be.
Objectives – the starting point for decision making. They state in general terms what the organisation wants to be able to achieve in the long term. They are important for planning and decision making.

 Mission statement, pages 22 and 23

Table 1.6 *Spot the difference!*

A word analysis of 300 mission statements showed that the following words were used:

Service	230 times
Customers	211 times
Quality	194 times
Value	183 times
Environment	104 times
Best	102 times

Mission Impossible

At the top of the list of objectives an organisation will have a mission statement. In theory this is meant to guide, inspire and remind but in practice many are uninspiring, long and so generally they do not actually mean much.

Among the main problems with typical mission statements are:

- it is very difficult to differentiate between them; for example, almost all state that the organisation wants to be best at something
- organisations are more concerned about their competitors' and customers' views rather than using them to improve effectiveness, e.g. 'in the future we will be seen as …'
- they state the obvious, e.g. 'we will provide value for money/high quality goods' and so on
- they are not always accurate.

Want to know more?

Another analysis, this time of 393 annual reports, showed:

- 16% of annual reports contained a mission statement
- 91% of mission statements were aimed at customers
- 60% referred to growth/profits or targets for shareholders
- 66% included statements aimed at staff
- 16% mentioned suppliers.

ACTIVITY

Go to the library or use the Internet and find five annual statements or reports from large organisations. If there are none there, write to ten large companies asking for a copy or try the websites of the same companies. How many of the reports contain mission statements?

Analyse the mission statements to find the following information:

1 The number of times the following words are used: service, customers, quality, value, environment, best.
2 Who are the statements aimed at?
3 Do a quick survey targeting a famous company familiar to everyone and try to find out if people are generally aware of mission statements and what they are.
4 Does your school or college have a mission statement? Do you know what it is? Do the staff know what it is? Try them! Does it contain any of the words in Table 1.6? Conduct a survey of parents, staff and students to see how many of them know what the mission statement is.
5 Devise a mission statement for your course. It will need to be short, sharp and snappy. Why not have a small prize for the best one? If the college or school uses it don't forget to put a price on it such as a new book in the library or a computer game!

A good mission statement should contain:
- Purpose – where you are going? It should not say that the company will be the best but that the company aims to be the best.
- Approach – how the company will achieve its purpose.
- Target group(s) – who you are aiming at with the statement?
- Measurable objectives – e.g. how large a market share? How much value will be added?
- Good language – negatives should be avoided. Sentences should be short and memorable.

An organisation's structure is driven by its mission and objectives. As we have seen, these vary from time to time. Operational objectives provide more detailed targets for the individual departments or sections. They are set and achieved by the organisation's management. The closer you get to the top of the organisation, the more likely you are to be working with the strategic objectives whilst workers lower down will be more concerned with operational objectives.

If an organisation has understandable and meaningful objectives everyone will have a clear sense of purpose and direction. Staff will be motivated by creating unity through working towards the same goals. The top management will be able to co-ordinate activities more effectively to achieve the objectives, and improvements in performance can be measured. For example, if a company's objective is to increase its profits by 10 per cent but it only makes a 5 per cent increase this objective will not have been achieved. Similarly a retail chain may state that one of its key objectives is to increase its number of stores by 12 per cent over the next three years. Everyone in the organisation will then be given operational objectives to contribute to this; for example, the Personnel Manager may be tasked with recruiting and training sufficient new staff, or the purchasing department will be required to increase the supply of products in order to fill the new stores. (See Figure 1.11.)

Who does what in an organisation?

In a small business different functions or roles such as finance, production, human resource management, marketing, operations, administration, and research and development may all be carried out by the same person. As businesses expand they employ specialists to carry out each of these functions.

As a business grows further, it will have departments for each of these functions. For instance, there may be a marketing department with a number of staff in it, each of whom has a different specialism such as sales, advertising or public relations. Eventually a business may have different departments for each of these different specialisms. In the very largest companies each separate area of the business (for instance, each separate product range or geographical area) may have its own specialist departments with a central administration department which pulls together the activities of all the different areas.

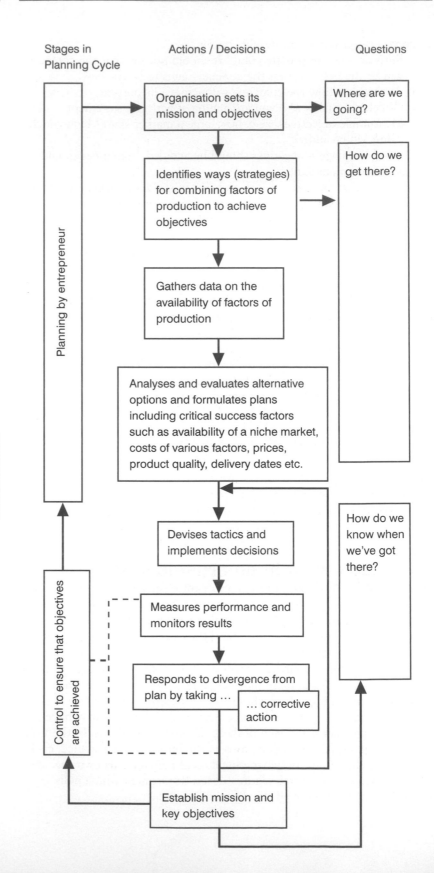

Key term

Niche market – finding a part of the market to specialise in, e.g. Costa Coffee, Tie Rack.

Figure 1.11 *Turning objectives into results*

Key functions

- **Finance** plans, records and monitors the flow of money in and out of the business.
- **Production** uses resources such as materials and labour to make goods or provide services.
- **Human resource management** (HRM) ensures that the people who work in the organisation are both fully employed and developed so that the business gets the best from them.
- **Marketing** identifies, anticipates and satisfies customer demands to achieve the objectives of the business. It includes advertising, selling and sales promotion, marketing research, introduction of new products or services, pricing, packaging, distribution and after-sales service.
- **Administration** uses systems to organise, co-ordinate and manage the running of businesses.
- **Research and development** is any activity which leads to new or improved technical knowledge about the products, processes, materials or working methods of the business.

Table 1.7 Launching a new product – how business functions interact

Decision	Function	Activity
What new flavour ice creams might our customers like?	Marketing	Market research
How do we create these flavours?	Research and development	Product design
What equipment and staffing would we need to make it?	Production	Production planning
How much might we sell the new flavour for?	Marketing	Market research
Would it make a profit?	Finance	Costing and financial planning
Should we make this new flavour?	Administration (management)	Decision-making
Do we have the staff we need? How can we get them?	Human resource management	Manpower planning, recruitment and selection, training
Do we have the materials and equipment we need to make the new ice cream?	Production	Purchasing
How can we make our customers want to buy this new flavour?	Marketing	Product promotion
How will we get this product to our customers?	Marketing	Distribution

Any activity or decision will involve specialists from all the different functions working together. Table 1.7 shows how many different functions need to be involved in deciding whether to launch a new product.

It is often difficult to understand the purpose of administration within a business since not many businesses still have departments called 'Administration', whereas most have departments called after each of the other functions. Even so, it is important since it is often the case that the administrative systems link the different functions together, enabling them to work together effectively. In any organisation the functions are combined and co-ordinated to enable the business to work effectively and efficiently.

CASE STUDY

Boots the Chemist

Matching supply to demand

Rod Scibbins, Director of Logistics at Boots the Chemist, realised that its strength lay in an integrated process, which would be committed to supporting stores at a consistently high level of service and at a viable cost; supply was just too important to Boots the Chemist to exist as a series of separate activities. So by combining warehousing and distribution with supply into a more cohesive logistics function Boots was reaping the benefits. He argues that 'we now have the largest and most complex operation in Europe. There's a high and ever changing inventory range in stores which vary in size from 50+ square metres to 4,200 square metres, with different stores stocking different ranges. In addition, we have the challenge of supplying the same product to stores with vastly different selling areas and patterns combined with the demands of providing a daily service on dispensing items as well. Efficiency and accuracy are key to our success.'

Source: CRAC Casebook 1996 Supply Chain Management

Made to fit? How organisations structure themselves

The structure of an organisation has an important impact on the character and culture of a business and on the attitudes and behaviour of people working in it. Most organisations show their internal structure and the way it operates with an organisation chart. This shows how the work in the organisation is divided up and carried out by individual groups and departments as well as how it is co-ordinated to achieve company goals and objectives. All organisations have different structures and the purpose of the structure seems to vary depending on whether you are the people who have designed it, or have to manage it, or have to work within it. Organisation charts show how jobs are grouped within the business. Depending on the size of the business, jobs will be grouped into sections, sections into units, units into departments and then into co-ordinated departments. Jobs can be grouped in several different ways.

Product or service

This structure is often used where there are many different products or services within the same organisation and each product or service is managed separately. It allows managers to group together the resources they need to make each product. For example, the Dixons Group has separate structures for each of its different chains of stores. This enables the company to concentrate on targeting different markets with each chain.

Figure 1.12

Function

In this type of structure, people and resources are grouped together depending on their function such as personnel, production, marketing. Often a large group such as the Dixons Group will have a functional structure within each of its different product groupings. For instance, PC World has its own organisational structure which is functional. The advantage of this type of structure is that it is generally more cost-effective to keep all specialists of a particular type together in one department rather than spreading them out thinly. It also enables more specialisms. For instance, within a Personnel Department, an organisation may be able to have specialist trainers, recruiters, employment law experts and so forth. If the organisation tried to allocate one personnel specialist to each of its functions, each personnel officer would have to have some knowledge of each personnel activity but expertise in none.

Figure 1.13

Customer

In sales-focused organisations the structure is often designed around different types of customers. Staff and resources are allocated to different customer groups. This enables everyone from research and production staff through to finance and personnel staff to concentrate on the needs of those particular clients. For instance, most banks are structured by client grouping – typically there may be different sections of the bank concentrating on personal customers (you and me), small business customers and large corporate customers.

Place/territory

This is used where the service is most economically provided within a specific area. For instance, the cost of shipping products from one country or region to another may mean that a business has separate operations in each area. A typical example of this is Coca-Cola, which is made in almost every country in which it is sold. It also allows customers much better access to the business. For this reason some sales-based organisations are structured around regional sales territories. Another reason for having geographically distinct operations is that they are then able to respond better to the different culture or environment in each region.

Figure 1.14 Coca-Cola ('Coca-Cola' and 'Coke' are registered trademarks of The Coca-Cola Company and are reproduced with kind permission from The Coca-Cola Company.)

ⓒASE STUDY

Eat, drink and be funny

Cultural mistakes

When a business has an organisational structure based on place or territory, it is much more likely to employ local staff rather than moving staff about from one region to another. This helps to avoid some of the pitfalls of doing business with people from a different culture.

Steve Morris offers this advice to business people trying to establish a good working relationship with customers in Kazakhstan.

'Food is central to the building of relationships. … You must eat or risk giving offence. … Americans seem to have upset the Kazakhs when they visited the country in the early 1990s. The Kazakhs got the impression that they did not like the food. The truth was that the Americans tended not to accept invitations to eat "at home" with their hosts. This is a big mistake.'

Source: *Professional Manager*, November 1999

▶ **Global communications, page 37**

| Relationships within an organisation

When a business is small most people will have to do a bit of everything: keep the accounts, sell the products and even make them. As businesses expand and become more complex they employ specialists to perform each of these functions. These individuals are often referred to as service providers.

Line, staff and functional relationships

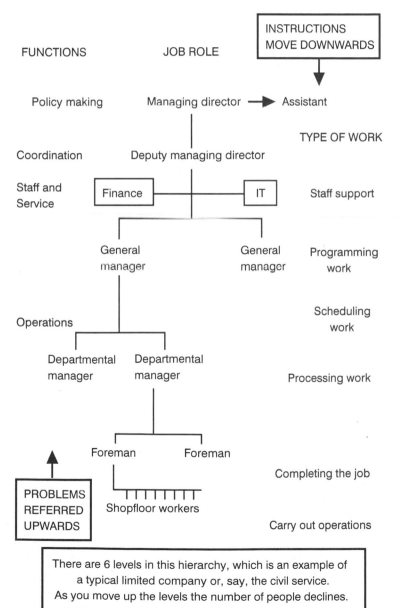

Figure 1.15 Hierarchical organisational structure

Line relationship

Each employee reports to a more senior person in the organisation. Figure 1.15 shows how people at each level of the organisation are linked through their authority to direct the activities of more junior staff. The departmental manager has the authority to direct the activities of the supervisors. In turn he or she can be directed by the general manager above him/her.

Staff relationship

Individuals who offer specialist advice on, for example, finance, computing or personnel have no authority on their own but act in the name of their superior and on his or her authority. In Figure 1.15 the managing director has an assistant with just such a relationship. They can offer advice and support but they do not have the authority to insist that the advice is taken. Because they are not in a line relationship they frequently do not constitute a level in the hierarchy.

Functional relationship

This is where a specialist provides a service which line managers are forced to accept. The general manager in Figure 1.15 may decide that the finance person can issue procedures directly to departmental managers. The functional specialist is accountable to the person in whose name he/she issues the instruction.

Similarly if a manager requires training for his or her staff then the organisational chart would show the relationship between the training specialist, the manager and the staff. The manager will have to delegate some of his or her own authority to the specialist to make it happen.

The people at the top (managing directors, chief executives) start a chain of command which passes from them through each manager to the various employees. Decisions, orders and instructions come down through this mechanism whilst information on which further decisions are made such as sales revenue and production costs are passed up the chain of command or hierarchy.

Flat and tall organisational structures

The number of levels of management between the top and the bottom of the organisational structure indicates whether it is flat or tall. Many UK companies have taken out whole layers of management in order to reduce costs in their attempt to become more responsive to their customers and markets. The argument is that companies with many levels create bureaucracy which prevents decisions from being made quickly and efficiently.

All hierarchies have to consider the span of control of each manager or supervisor. Each manager in a tall organisation controls a relatively small number of employees compared with a manager in a flat structure.

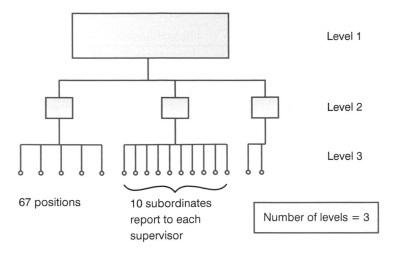

Figure 1.16 Flat organisational structure

Organisations with a flat structure have very few levels of authority. Figure 1.16 shows that only one level of hierarchy separates the managing director from the employees.

Organisations with a tall structure have many levels of authority. Figure 1.17 shows four levels separating the managing director and the employees.

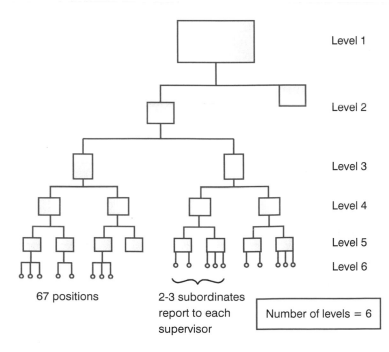

Figure 1.17 Tall organisational structure

Table 1.8 *Advantages and disadvantages of tall organisational structures*

Advantages	Disadvantages
More promotion opportunities	Slower communication between top and bottom
Clear line management structure	May be less responsibility and authority for middle managers
Clear division of responsibility and allocation of authority	May reduce motivation and job satisfaction at the bottom
Greater control over employees from the top	Working across departments may be more difficult

Hierarchical and matrix structures

Sometimes, organisations will have a structure that is either hierarchical or matrix, or a mixture of both. In hierarchical structures the lines of responsibility and authority are clear with each employee reporting to one specific manager (see Figure 1.15).

In matrix structures employees find that they report to several different managers or supervisors for different aspects of their jobs (see Figure 1.18).

The hierarchical structure is more common but an increasing number of companies are using matrix structures to manage projects. Where this occurs, a company selects people from a number of different departments to work together on a project. For instance, to design and launch a new product, people from production, finance, computer services and marketing might work together. Within the project team they would be reporting to the project leader but for the other aspects of their jobs they would be reporting to their heads of department (e.g. the production manager).

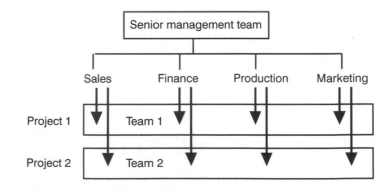

Emphasis is on team work and participation

Figure 1.18 *Matrix organisational structure*

Table 1.9 *Advantages and disadvantages of matrix structures*

Advantages	Disadvantages
Easier to manage projects	Lines of authority and responsibility may be unclear
Enables people from different departments to work together	Can increase bureaucracy and administrative costs
Encourages more flexibility in employees	Can lead to conflicting demands for time and loyalty of employees
Reduces number of specialists required	

Centralised and decentralised organisations

The control within organisations can either be concentrated centrally or spread amongst the various sections of the business. Where control is centralised, decision making, authority and responsibility are all focused on the small number of people at the top of the organisation. In a decentralised organisation a much greater number of people participate in decision making.

The extent to which there is centralisation is one of the main influences over the organisation's management style.

Table 1.10 *Advantages and disadvantages of centralised organisations*

Advantages	Disadvantages
Control is held by the most experienced and senior people in the organisation	Employees may feel more motivated if they are involved in the decision-making process
Communication between decision-makers will be fast and easy	Decision-makers may be remote from what is actually happening
Decisions can be made quickly	Middle managers may not be trained to make decisions
Employees are not pressurised into taking responsibility	Senior managers may feel the strain of being responsible for all the decision-making

| Management styles

For managers to be effective they need to adopt a style of management which suits the structure and culture of the organisations in which they work. It is also important that a manager is able to change his or her style of management depending on the situation. It used to be thought that each person only had one natural style of management and that they would use it in any situation. Current theories of leadership identify

> **Key terms**
>
> **Managers** plan, organise and monitor the work performed by others in order to carry out the tasks for which they are responsible.

the most effective managers as those who can adapt the way they manage to the type of employees involved, the nature of the task to be done and the structure in which they are working.

There are four main styles of management which are recognised as being effective if used at the right time.

Autocratic

Managers who adopt an autocratic style of management will take full responsibility for everything and keep all their authority to themselves. They will tell their staff what to do and how to do it and will expect to be obeyed without discussion.

Consultative

Managers who are consultative discuss most issues with their staff but retain overall control. Managers will listen to what their team has to say but will usually make the decisions themselves.

Democratic

Managers using a democratic (or participative) style will delegate some authority to their teams so that the teams are able to make decisions themselves. Where the managers retain control they still discuss decisions fully with their staff and are heavily influenced by their opinions.

Laissez faire

Managers who adopt a laissez faire style have delegated all their authority to their team. They believe that the team is capable of making all the necessary decisions itself. The manager then concentrates on co-ordinating the team's activities and representing the team in its communication with other teams and senior management.

Some writers have linked each management style to a different situation in order to identify when each management style should be adopted. The deciding factors are the ability, willingness and confidence of the people who are being managed.

Ⓒ ASE STUDY

Which style would you prefer?

Early in 1997 a MORI poll asked 1,700 people if they would like to give up their jobs. Sixty-four per cent said yes, if they could afford to. Only 20 per cent said they really enjoyed their work. Most surveys that ask what management approaches result in satisfied and well motivated employees find that most people prefer decentralised, democratic structures to centralised autocratic structures.

Michelle Green

24, team leader of the sales department of 'Loot' London

'I enjoy my job because the company really cares about the staff. One of the major perks is that once a week we're entitled to a back massage. The whole office has been designed ergonomically and we have a health and safety officer who does monthly assessments to check we're sitting properly etc. We also get eye tests, and free fruit in the afternoon. Every day at 3 p.m. there's a delivery, and the expenditure goes into thousands of pounds for the year. The chairman wants everyone to be healthy.'

Aston Lewin

35, production supervisor, Grain D'Or Bakeries, Northern Foods

'I'm in charge of the people on the shop floor who make croissants. We turn out about one million a week. The people are from all different backgrounds – Sri Lankans, Indians, Somalians – and I enjoy learning from their cultures. The company is good at recognising people who want to get on – race doesn't make any difference. The Bakers Union has had access for the past three years and now that membership has reached over 50 per cent they are going to put together a union recognition agreement.'

Jo Da Silva

30, consultant constructual engineer, Ove Arup & Partners

'One of the reasons I became an engineer was because someone told me that engineers build bridges, and I thought how nice it would be to look at something and know you helped build it. Doing that is the buzz of the job. It's a very creative job, but it's a down-to-earth creativity. I like working best on public buildings. I helped design Stansted Airport and have done work on London Underground. I have skills that are really useful and I sleep easy at night. If I was doing it just for money, I wouldn't like it so much.'

David Chisholm

28, The Bristol Steiner Waldorf School

'At the Steiner school we work closely with children's thoughts, feelings and emotions. As a teacher, you have one class for eight years – from seven to 14 – and I get a lot of job satisfaction from watching them develop. The children don't have conventional lessons and I enjoy being able to bring subjects to them in different ways. The children learn through song, poetry and writing. Some children who have come into the class have found the state system difficult and, because the way we work here is very different, it is satisfying to watch them flourish.'

Source: *The Big Issue*, 10 November 1997

Are you woman enough to be boss?

In 1999, *Management Today* conducted an extensive survey of male and female managers. Their findings suggested that many of the characteristics seen as 'feminine' (e.g. considerate, open-minded, good team player) were as essential in a modern manager as the more traditional 'male' characteristics (e.g. decisiveness, team leading).

'After years of women having to suppress their natural behaviour in the workplace, our findings show that the pendulum is swinging the other way. A plausible argument can now be made that men need to find and express their more feminine characteristics to be successful leaders in the new millennium. The future need not be female, but it is certainly feminine – at least when it comes to such leadership skills as praising staff, managing time and being seen as more trustworthy and solicitous.'

Source: *Management Today*, October 1999

Communication in organisations

Communication is central to the style of any manager and important to employees. If people know clearly what their managers expect of them they are more likely to contribute to the achievement of the organisation's objectives. Autocratic management styles rely on giving instructions and obtaining information whereas more democratic styles depend on much more complex forms of communication.

You are going on your first 'business trip' abroad and you want to make sure everything goes well. You will obviously need to pack your latest outfits and you probably try in vain to get everything into your suitcase. But you're not going on holiday! You may not even get to see the country!

Supposing this first trip is to Egypt, what sort of things will you need to consider? Make a list of the following:

1 Essential reference material
2 Essential basic skills you will need
3 Useful websites
4 Dates to avoid meetings
5 Cultural information

Make sure you've read the case study below. Have you got everything covered?

Ⓐ CTIVITY

Divide yourselves into small groups of about six or seven people. Take about one hour and invent a culture from scratch, deciding on your own norms and values. Ask your teacher if you can video the results. While you are watching everyone's contributions, think what you learn about body language and power games. Who, for instance, dominates the proceedings and why? Who hasn't said much? Why? Is it part of their culture?

Increasingly many companies pay attention to this kind of detail. They have to ensure they do not lose potential business. If you've thought about these questions you will be better prepared for your first business trip.

Ⓒ ASE STUDY

Being a global communicator

Knowing your customer

During a trade mission to Japan, the Prime Minister, Tony Blair, caused consternation to the local interpreters by using the phrase 'going the full Monty'. You can just imagine them thinking, 'thanks, Tony, but this is not in our English–Japanese dictionaries!'

We tend to think that English is the universal language and if we are not understood then we simply speak louder and slower. A Norwegian will have no problem understanding a German who speaks to her in English, but because the British aren't accustomed to simplifying their use of English they frequently leave their international listeners at sea. Similarly, silence matters too. Many Westerners hate gaps in the conversation. In some Scandinavian countries silence may indicate respect for the previous speaker. 'He who speaks is a dumb ass', as one Japanese saying goes.

Figure 1.19 Knowing your customer

We are all part of a global economy, linked together by telecoms and videocoms. We need to achieve core skills that will enable us to work across language and cultural barriers.

Want to know more?

Useful websites: Foreign and Commonwealth Office: www.fco.gov.uk
British Chambers of Commerce: www.britishchambers.org.uk
BBC Languages: www.bbc.co.uk/education/languages/
Centre for Information on Language Teaching and Research: www.cilt.org.uk

Working across cultures

- **Invest time and money in learning foreign languages.** Being able to speak a few simple phrases of greeting and appreciation in several languages shows courtesy and goes a long way in business. It shows commitment to meeting your contacts on their own ground.

- **Appreciate cultural diversity.** People behave differently throughout the world. Some cultures use touch more than others whilst others take a while to build up trust.

- **Read as much as you can about other cultures.** You will come across values which you are not familiar with. Hold a group discussion to compare your cultural values with those of others in your group. This will identify how diverse they are in a typical school or college, let alone another country.

- **Understand body language.** We need to be aware of how our body language is interpreted. Avoid making judgements. If someone looks away when you are speaking it doesn't necessarily mean they are a bit shifty; it may be that their culture regards sustained eye contact as aggressive behaviour.

- **Check dress codes** of the country you are working in.

How to communicate

Communication is vital to any organisation if it is to achieve its objectives. It enables people to understand what tasks they have to carry out and why, and it allows businesses to check whether they are meeting their objectives. Team members rely on information that others provide. Problem solving, decision making or reaching agreement requires team members to exchange information and this usually has to come through a chain or network of people.

CASE STUDY

Business communication

Question: Communication is vital in any business. But how much of what we pick up from what people tell us is verbal?

Answer: Only 7 per cent of what is perceived from communication is verbal; 38 per cent is derived from paralinguistics (style, manner, tone, medium) and 55 per cent from body language.

Source: *The Observer*, 30 August 1998

Channels of communication

The evidence shows that management styles affect the type of communication used by organisations. Autocratic management styles tend to use wheels or chains whereas democratic styles use comcon or circles. The laissez-faire style produces a more fragmented approach to communication.

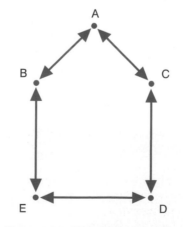

Figure 1.20 *Circle communication systems*

Figure 1.21 *Comcon communication systems*

In centralised organisations members go through someone at the centre of the communication network. This means that not everybody has equal access to the information. In decentralised organisations information is shared more freely between members and access to information is more equal. It is interesting to note that simple tasks performed on centralised networks are done much more quickly and accurately. Decentralised communications systems produce faster and more accurate performance with complex tasks.

Job satisfaction is greater where there is more participation in decision making and members of the team are more equal.

Open and restricted channels

If you want to communicate with everybody you can use e-mail, posters, magazines and notice boards. Anyone who reads them gets the information. One problem with this is that some people will not bother to read them. However, most communications are restricted since access is limited. When managers are planning to move the factory location they won't want the workforce to know about their plans until all the negotiations are complete. Similarly, when companies are launching new products or services they try to keep them secret to prevent competitors copying their ideas.

Some information will always be restricted, such as personnel records, salaries and bank details. Managers face the challenge of deciding what information should be open and what should be restricted and how much information they should share with the workforce. Staff in some organisations complain about communication overload and find it difficult to select the information they really need to do their job. In other organisations the common complaint is that information is so restricted that staff do not know enough to do their jobs effectively. Many people regard knowledge as power and there is a danger in more autocratic organisations that information will be withheld by managers to make them feel more in control.

Verbal/non-verbal

Besides deciding how much information to pass on, everyone in the organisation needs to decide how best to send the information to the recipient. Verbal forms of communication, such as face-to-face conversations, meetings, telephone calls and video-conferencing, have the advantages of being fast and of allowing immediate feedback. It is often a more difficult form of communication since it requires both oral and active listening skills.

Non-verbal forms of communication, such as reports, letters, memos, e-mail, fax and bulletins, enable the sender and the recipient to keep a record and are useful when complex information needs to be communicated. However, they are usually a slower means of communicating and the sender has no immediate feedback as to whether the message has been received and understood. Most

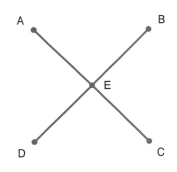

Figure 1.22 *Wheel communication systems*

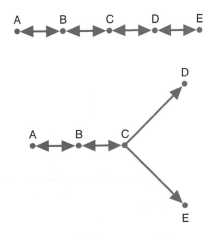

Figure 1.23 *Chain communications systems*

39

organisations rely heavily on non-verbal communication, which means that staff may not read everything they receive.

Sometimes managers choose to use non-verbal communications in a situation where they want to avoid face-to-face contact with other staff since such contact is more likely to lead to their authority or decisions being questioned or to emotionally difficult situations where the information to be communicated is not going to be well received. Effective communication relies on choosing the right times to use verbal and non-verbal methods and on having the right communications network and organisation structure.

ⒸASE STUDY

Chinese Whispers

Figure 1.24

A factory employing 1,200 staff had a highly hierarchical structure and suffered from severe communication problems. Things which managers had intended to be firm instructions became advice or guidance by the time they reached the shop floor. This was a particular problem where the communication was verbal since each layer of the hierarchy reinterpreted or diluted the instructions – remember Chinese Whispers? Similarly, communications upwards suffered from dilution as each level of management tried to communicate in terms that would least offend the manager above. The Chief Executive tried solving this problem in the following way. He bypassed the managers and communicated directly with the workers by visiting the shop floor daily and participating in their work. This did not work because it did not solve the problem of the need for specific information to be passed up and down the organisation daily. In fact it made it worse since the managers and supervisors who had to pass on this information were no longer regarded by the workers as part of the communication network. If the Chief Executive had wanted to solve the problem by more direct communication he should first have reduced the number of managerial levels.

I heard it through the grapevine!

Official instructions use formal channels of communication to pass information. All organisations have informal channels of communication alongside the formal ones. These are often called the grapevine and are often as powerful as formal channels, and e-mail makes communication through the grapevine more sophisticated and faster.

Informal communication channels can be a key element in an organisation's structure. They are one of the most effective ways of spreading the culture of the organisation and developing relationships between staff. Some companies try to prevent informal communication because it is not controlled from the top. Where this occurs, the grapevine goes underground and is much more likely to spread inaccurate and hostile information. Informal communication will never be stopped. It always occurs whenever people take breaks from their work or meet each other in a more relaxed situation. The management of an effective organisation uses the grapevine to its benefit. Managers can gauge people's feelings about situations from what is being said on the grapevine and can use it to leak information unofficially. Government departments sometimes leak information to journalists through informal channels so that they can assess public opinion before making a formal announcement.

What happens if communication goes wrong?

Communications don't just happen, they have to be worked at. Charles Handy, an experienced management expert, made the following observations about communications 'fall-out':

- A study of the production department of a British firm found that a department manager recorded himself as having given 165 instructions or decisions. In the same period his deputies recorded receiving instructions on only 84 of those occasions, a fall-out of nearly 50 per cent.
- A study at Columbia University discovered that the retention of content matter at the end of a lecture was only 50 per cent – a figure that dropped to 25 per cent after two weeks.
- A study of information dissemination in 100 United States firms found that, of information disseminated by the president of the organisation, the first level down recalled receiving only 63 per cent, the third level only 40 per cent and the fifth level only 20 per cent.

There are obviously lots of difficulties in communicating effectively.

- Receivers of information may hear what they want to hear rather than what you are telling them.

- You may not be giving the message clearly enough for everyone to understand it. You may be using language that others do not understand or you may be communicating in a confused fashion.

- Senders of information may deliberately withhold information or issue misleading information to further their own ambitions rather than those of the organisation.

- People do not always believe what they hear or say what they really mean because they do not trust one another.

No wonder organisations both large and small have so many problems with communication.

If only half of what you say is heard or remembered, can you be sure which half it is?

How is information technology affecting communications?

Although the use of information and communications technology is widespread there is a mistaken view that it is mostly about faster ways of doing the same job. For instance, a spreadsheet package allows a business to calculate its profit forecasts much more quickly. When people predict the effects of IT, it is usually in terms of relatively simple situations such as a reduction in the need for secretarial staff or a greater ability to work from home. Whilst these may or may not be likely to happen as a result of the spread of information technology, what is having more impact is the complete change to the nature of the work. The improvements in communication are making the acquisition of knowledge faster and easier.

It's not what you know!

According to Professor of Management, Peter Drucker, 'The basic economic resource is no longer capital, nor natural resources nor labour. It is and it will be knowledge.' When your teachers or lecturers were at school the emphasis was probably on acquiring as much knowledge as possible. Exam-based qualifications confirmed the view that what was important was that you could prove how much knowledge you had at your fingertips. You probably still find that much of what you do at school or college is learn facts. However, more emphasis is now given to how you manage those facts.

Consider your own course – you can succeed by showing that you have acquired some knowledge and have managed to apply it to a particular situation (through your assessment activities). However, to get a better grade you have to demonstrate quite advanced knowledge management skills such as identifying what you need to know, working out how to acquire that knowledge and deciding how to use it to solve a challenge.

It is these knowledge management skills that businesses are increasingly looking for from their employees. In the USA many of the larger companies already have 'CKOs' (Chief Knowledge Officers) in senior management positions. In the UK, the Government's White Paper 'Our competitive future: Building the knowledge driven economy' recognised the communication revolution caused by information technology. If you have access to the Internet you may well have already discovered that almost anything you want to know can be found there – the trick is knowing how to find it! Likewise, e-mail, faxes, mobile phones, v-commerce based on voice recognition technology and audio- and video-conferencing mean you can communicate worldwide almost instantaneously, and increasingly cheaply.

In some respects the challenge for businesses in the future will be too much information. The most that successful businesses will be able to do is decide what information is important and use that information for decision making. However, they will also have to ensure that their communication systems are strong enough to enable prompt and full sharing of knowledge to avoid duplication of effort on the one hand and, on the other, a gaping void when the employee with the know-how leaves. Information technology has an important role to play in improving communications, although it is not necessarily a complete substitute for more traditional forms of communication.

Ⓒ ASE STUDY

Knowing what you know

Technology is not the only way to share and create knowledge. Get-togethers such as breakfast briefings or away-days can provide a forum to exchange lessons learned in different parts of the business. Consulting firm, Smythe Dorward Lambert, has a 'wall of knowledge' in its kitchen area where anybody can post useful material relating to their work.

Source: *Management Today*, November 1999

Ⓒ ASE STUDY

Youth rules, OK?

The next generation

Many experts predict that in the near future the corporate website will not just be an interesting sideline to the 'real' business of an organisation. Instead it will be the organisation's living centre, an interactive hub linking all a business's stakeholders, and the key to its success or failure. If this happens, many companies will find themselves effectively dependent on a different type of workforce. Who will be this workforce? Many experts believe they will not be the gentlemen in suits from the boardroom floor, who don't know their HTTP from their HTML. It will be the 'N' or Net Generation of those at school or college who will dominate this key aspect of business. In the US, children as young as 10 are earning up to $80 an hour designing websites. In the UK, ICL is headhunting children as young as 14 as the future generation of cyber commanders and web mistresses.

ⒸASE STUDY

It's good to talk – the future of business communications

But can he win the National Lottery?

British Telecom, like most businesses in the communications industry, is so dependent upon being able to anticipate future developments that it employs Ian Pearson as a futurologist. His job is to look into the future, keeping track of developments throughout technology and figuring out the future implications for BT and its customers. This is hardly an exact science. As Ian says, 'Accuracy is impossible for all but the most trivial question, but blurred vision is better than none at all.'

Visit his pages on http://innovate.bt.com to see his predictions on everything from Christmas 50 years from now to what work will be like in ten years' time.

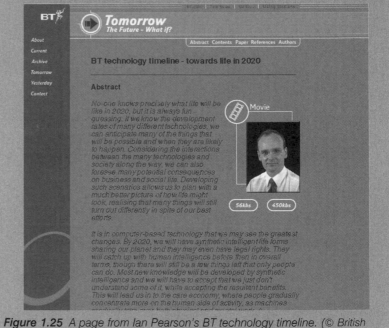

Figure 1.25 A page from Ian Pearson's BT technology timeline. (© British Telecommunications plc 1999, reproduced with permission.)

The internet and e-mail

Information technology is changing our patterns of communication. However, this change is not happening as fast as you might think. Recent research shows that 64 per cent of the UK's smaller businesses do not have access to the Internet. Only 22 per cent have websites and only

4 per cent make regular use of e-mail. Nevertheless, however small a business is, it cannot ignore the Internet for much longer. It is predicted that by 2002 there will be over 300 million potential users of the web and that the industry will be worth £184 billion. A business that does not use the web to actively market its products or services will be losing out in a major way.

Besides using the web for marketing, or for actually making sales, forward-looking businesses use it as a management tool, enabling them to communicate effectively between various sites and with both customers and suppliers. How many of you signed up for your course through your school or college's website?

CASE STUDY

KMA

Using the technology to communicate

Fast-growing KMA Interactive Media Ltd is a dynamic young company employing eight people to produce award-winning interactive multimedia training packages.

Clients as diverse as Channel 4, Dow Chemical, Shell and the Arts Council have turned to it for web-based training courses that are custom-designed to meet their own unique requirements. When placed on a customer's central computer server, they are available throughout the organisation – and all over the world. 'People can study courses at their own speed and at times to suit themselves, but the client always knows exactly how they are progressing,' says KMA's creative director Kit Monkman. KMA's innovative use of technology strengthens the richness of its multimedia solutions. But technology also underpins how the company operates.

KMA's use of e-mail and teleconferencing plays a vital role in helping the company's designers and project managers stay close to clients' requirements. Content specialists and graphic artists from all over the country are linked through the Internet to form a virtual organisation. Even voice-overs arrive electronically: the script is sent via e-mail and the finished recording sent as a digital file.

'Clients really appreciate the fact that we can use the best people, irrespective of where they are,' enthuses Monkman. 'We in turn value our ability to stay in touch with clients, wherever they happen to be.' Soon, KMA's website will bring those links even closer, with clients being able to go online to examine work-in-progress, check on project milestones, and review how many hours each project is consuming.

'We're not a large organisation at all,' says Monkman. 'But technology allows us to out-punch our weight.'

Source: *Management Today*, October 1999

Audio- and video-conferencing

Potentially one of the most influential changes in business communication outside of the Internet will be the growth in audio- and video-conferencing. These are very powerful tools in bringing people together without them having to leave their desks. Already audio-conferencing is available even through your home telephone system and is widely used in business. Video-conferencing is not as extensively used but we've heard of lots of companies who use it regularly, particularly for international links and discussions. Don't forget the company saves all those airfares, hotel bills and other expenses! To provide good quality links expensive ISDN lines and high quality cameras are required. Even so, developments in IT have made video links via your desktop computer widely available.

Audio- and video-conferencing can be used to improve communications in a number of ways:

- Regular meetings – a business can schedule, for instance, a regular morning briefing session for all its sales staff without them having to travel to a central office. Where, as is often the case, the salesforce is widely distributed such meetings would be impossible otherwise.

- Instant meetings – when a new opportunity or problem arises, a business may need to consult a number of people quickly before a decision is made. For instance, a customer may telephone with a request for a special order. The business may need to hold a discussion between the customer, the production manager, the sales manager and the finance department before it is able to decide whether to take the order.

- Presentations – video-conferencing is particularly useful when colleagues or customers can see an actual demonstration of ideas or products. Some advertising agencies use this method to present new

Businesses who regularly use audio- or video-conferencing identify a number of important benefits.

- **Reductions in the costs of time taken for travel** (not to mention the environmental benefits of using transport less)

- **Improved availability of staff**

- **More relaxed approach to meetings** with people comfortable in their own offices

- **Immediate access to paperwork**, etc on participants' own desktop or computer

- **Through international telecommunications networks and mobile phones, conferencing is available for almost anywhere in the world**

- **Faster dissemination of information**

- **Faster response times**

- **Faster and more-informed decision-making**

- **Stronger links with customers and suppliers.**

However, critics argue that something important is lost when communication is not face to face. Given what was said earlier about the importance of non-verbal communication, there may be a reduction in the effectiveness of communication by remote means. For this reason, perhaps audio- and video-conferencing should be seen as an enhancement to more traditional conferencing methods, not as a complete replacement.

Figure 1.26 Improving communications with video-conferencing

concepts to their clients. Although it loses some of the personal touch, it does enable them to consult clients at every stage of the process.

- Remote training – some businesses now use video-conferencing to train members of their workforce who are spread over a wide geographic area. It is sometimes used with a large group of trainees in much the same format as a traditional lesson but with interaction via cameras and screens rather than with trainers and trainees in the same room. It is also used to provide face-to-face feedback or advice to individual trainees. One college uses this method to provide assessment and feedback on demand to employees in a bank's call-centre who are taking courses in Customer Service.

- Project management – major projects often bring together a number of people from different companies or different branches who need to meet frequently to review the project and agree plans. Timberland, for instance, used audio-conferencing to plan a worldwide sales conference. Project members from various countries met regularly to organise the conference without having to travel to meetings.

- Remote expertise or advice – a typical example occurs in the construction industry. The Channel Tunnel Rail Link involved numerous construction sites strung out over a 50-mile route. Rather than have specialist structural engineers and geologists travelling from site to site, it was possible to locate them more centrally and have them deal with many of the problems remotely.

Organisational culture

This is a very important feature of organisations since it affects the behaviour of everyone in it. It is deeply embedded in the organisation and may be unaffected by the management. The culture of an organisation can only be changed in the long term. In fact, it may not be possible to change it at all.

What is organisational culture?

The culture of an organisation (also called Corporate Culture and Organisational Climate) is important because it affects many of the things we have already discussed. For instance:

- the style of management that the organisation uses
- people's awareness of each other within the organisation
- the structure of the organisation and how flexibly it adapts to the workload
- the attitudes and beliefs about what is right and what is wrong. These are frequently referred to as corporate values. This leads

"A quality of perceived organisational specialness – that it possesses some unusual quality that distinguishes it from others in the field." (Gold 1982)

"Culture … is a pattern of beliefs and expectations shared by the organisation's members. These beliefs and expectations produce norms that powerfully shape the behaviour of individuals and groups in the organisation." (Schwartz and Davis 1981)

"Culture is the commonly held and relatively stable beliefs, attitudes and values that exist within the organisation." (Williams, Dobson and Waiters 1993)

"The culture of the factory is its customary and traditional way of thinking and of doing things, which is shared to a greater or lesser degree by all its members, and which new members must learn, and at least partially accept, in order to be accepted into service in the firm. Culture in this sense covers a wide range of behaviours: the methods of production; job skills and technical knowledge; attitudes towards discipline and punishment; the customs and habits of managerial behaviour; the objectives of the concern; its way of doing business; the methods of payment; the values placed on different types of work; beliefs in democratic living and joint consultation; and the less conscious conventions and taboos." (Gaques 1952)

people to act and behave in particular ways and can be seen in:
1 the language people use
2 the stories and myths about the past
3 what is seen as acceptable behaviour in the workplace
4 the rules and customs of the organisation
5 heroes and role models.

Corporate culture affects business planning and strategy in a number of ways:

- how effectively the mission and corporate objectives are shared by all employees
- how decision-making processes and management styles are used
- whether employees are self starters and do not have to be supervised constantly
- whether the organisation is a risk taker
- whether the senior management team sees the organisation as a market leader or follower – is it conservative and traditional or forward looking and trend setting?
- whether the organisation has drive and energy.

As you can imagine more conservative cultures tend to go for low-risk strategies and rely on what they do best and what they know. They may have a tall organisation structure and autocratic management style. The employees like being associated with the company and there are certain attitudes and standards of behaviour expected of them.

 Hierarchy, pages 29–32

Communicating the business culture

Part of any business culture entails stories, myths and exaggerations. These are often based on past incidents, rumours, innuendo, the consequences of past mistakes and poor communication within an organisation. Communicating corporate culture begins from the day a person joins an organisation. New workers are keen to settle in and find their way in their job and the organisation. This will happen through formal methods such as training and informal methods such as observing role models and chatting over tea or coffee. For businesses it is a way of putting their mark on employees, whereas for the latter it is a matter of learning how to survive from day to day and develop in the future.

CASE STUDY

The positive and negative influences of culture

Table 1.11 *Interview with company employees about culture and its influence*

Positive +	Negative −
Employees have a sense of identity	Employees may be highly resistant to change
Have a clear framework within which to work	Highly bureaucratic
Have stable interpersonal relationships	Short sighted

An organisation's strategies will change regularly but its culture may not, despite changes in the structure of the organisation. However, many managers over the last few years have thought that they could do this – with disastrous consequences. British Airways suffered a large fall in profits in recent years, leading to the resignation of the Chief Executive in 2000. Some commentators argue that the business developed a negative culture which was partly caused by the company's redundancy programme in the late 1990s.

Types of culture

Charles Handy in *Understanding Voluntary Organisations* identified four basic cultures.

Club culture (power)

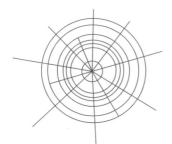

Figure 1.27 Spider's web

Handy illustrates it with a spider's web (see Figure 1.27). The key to the organisation is in the centre and it is characterised by an all-powerful boss or founder. There are not many rules, systems or committees.

'We don't have many memos, minutes of meetings and volumes of procedures. We don't have any committees either, which is great. All the decisions – well the big ones – are taken by the management. Decisions tend to be based on what we've done before or how we did it.'

These corporate cultures are 'rich in personality'. They abound with stories and folklore from the past when 'life was more exciting'. They can be very exciting and interesting places in which to work if you belong to the club and share the values and beliefs of the spider. The biggest danger of course is what happens without the spider.

Role culture

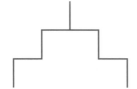

Figure 1.28 Pyramid structure

This culture is very bureaucratic and the organisation chart looks like a pyramid of boxes (see Figure 1.28). Job roles and descriptions are set and changes are made to them from time to time. There are set procedures, systems and rules for everything.

Communications are very formal – memos and minutes go from team leader to deputy to staff. Everything revolves around the rules and unspoken etiquette.

The organisation is managed rather than led. Initiative and independence are not encouraged and it may be essential that they aren't – would you want airline pilots to land an aircraft on the wrong runway because the view was more attractive for the passengers? These organisations are very secure and predictable but for these reasons they find it difficult to adapt to change.

The task culture

This is a job- or project-led organisation and tends to be linked with matrix-style structures (see Figure 1.29). The culture is task oriented and a team and resources are applied to a project, problem or task. People work in co-operative groups, thrive on challenge and change and generally have high levels of job satisfaction. This type of culture is often adopted by consultants, advertising agencies, construction teams, journalists, the media and surgical teams.

The person culture

This occurs where individual talents come first, such as with doctors, barristers, architects, etc., and is illustrated by the stellar structure (see Figure 1.30). Such organisations tend not to have managers but secretaries, bursars, chief clerks and so on. These organisations are difficult to run in the usual way. Professionals have to be persuaded, influenced, cajoled and bargained with, not managed.

Changing the corporate culture

Identifying the organisation's culture helps to understand why some people don't fit in. It also helps to explain how difficult it is to change a corporate culture. If you want change you may need to:

* appoint new staff
* encourage new working methods through incentive schemes
* improve communications between managers and workers
* promote staff who are energetic, flexible and have the right attitude
* encourage the participation and involvement of people who will be affected by the change.

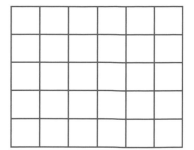

Figure 1.29 *Matrix structure*

Matrix structures, page 32

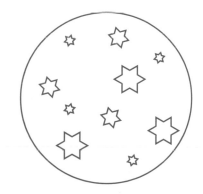

Figure 1.30 *Stellar structure*

| Production and quality

We have already considered how businesses combine the four factors of production (or inputs) to create output which could be sold at a profit (see Figure 1.31). Every organisation has its own set of outputs, which could be manufactured products such as food, car parts, houses, or garden furniture; they could be grown or mined from the earth; or they could be services such as banking, travel, or legal and accountancy services. In each situation the business converts a range of inputs into an output that someone else wants to buy. Businesses are able to make this profitable if the income they receive is greater than the cost of all the inputs.

Factors of production, page 2

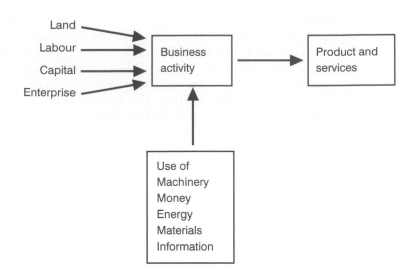

Figure 1.31 How inputs become converted into output

There are four main production processes, each of which transforms inputs into finished products:

- **extraction – e.g. mining**

- **analytic techniques – this breaks down existing materials to create another product, e.g. using cocoa beans to create chocolate**

- **fabrication – this involves the joining of two or more pieces of material, e.g. welding or clothes manufacturing**

- **synthesis – this is the creation of new materials or substances using a range of different materials or components, e.g. car production**

Added value, page 55

Adding value

One way for a business to be profitable is to combine factors of production in such a way as to make the finished product valuable. This allows the business to sell its products and earn a surplus. This process is one of adding value, i.e. the value of the output is greater than the costs of all the inputs. The greater the value that can be added, the higher the price that can be charged for the finished product.

An example may make this clearer. Airlines are in the business of flying passengers from A to B. This can be achieved in a variety of ways. It is to an airline's advantage if it can find ways that add value to customers' journeys as this makes the trip more pleasurable and allows the airline to charge a higher price. Airlines achieve this by:

- offering different types of seat with different degrees of comfort and space
- providing stewards and stewardesses to 'wait on' passengers
- providing 'free' drinks
- providing VIP and economy services in the airport terminal at the check-in, e.g. rest-rooms, showers, VIP lounges, etc.

But not all companies in the airline industry offer these additional facilities. While some businesses seek to add as many services as possible (for example, Virgin Airlines offers customers travelling first-class the option of a double bed on their London to New York flights), other companies have sought to reduce the number of frills. Businesses can be profitable without the extras.

The airline industry is a good example of how profits can be made either way: lower-priced seats without extras mean lower costs incurred by the airline and therefore increased profits. It is only worth providing the value-added services if customers are prepared to pay for them.

ACTIVITY

You have decided to have a 'gap' year before going to work full time or studying at university. With a couple of friends you'd like to travel to Australia in July, stopping over in the following places: Amsterdam, Athens, Dubai, Bangkok, Singapore, Hong Kong and finally arriving in Sydney. It doesn't matter how long it takes and you may well be able to add in some other interesting destinations en route. You want to go as cheaply as you can but you need to take care not to keep doubling back. Find out the prices for flying First class, Business class and Economy.

Can you find anything cheaper? Would it be better to have an 'all in one ticket'? How do services on board vary?

Draw up a table showing alternative routes and airlines together with prices. Which represents the best value? Why? Is the cheapest necessarily the best? Will you have to spend a lot of time waiting around in airports?

Don't forget to try some internet sites, such as:

www.buzzaway.com www.usitcampus.co.uk
www.telme.com www.britishmidland.com
www.statravel.co.uk www.lastminute.com

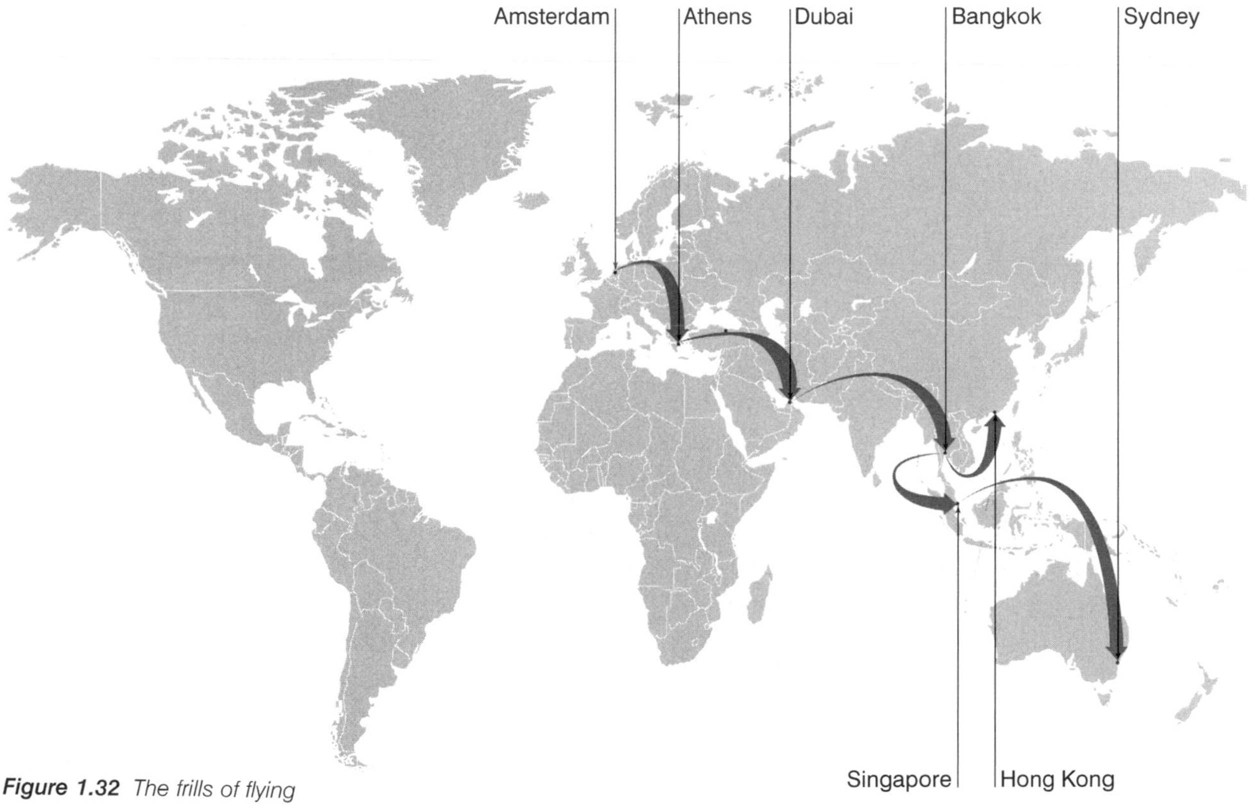

Figure 1.32 The frills of flying

(C)ASE STUDY

Model aeroplanes

All airlines are safe and just as fast as each other, but they do not all offer the same services. Some airlines only provide the bare essentials. These budget airlines provide a service with 'no frills' and usually fly to Europe and the USA. Some of the 'new' airlines offering a no-frills service include: Ryanair, Easyjet, Debonair, Go, Alitalia.

Even with the cut-throat competition in the airline industry, these low-cost operators are successful. Their success is built on low prices and meeting the needs of customers.

Figure 1.33 Model aeroplanes

Why do businesses want to add value?

The above example of low-cost airlines looks as if these companies do not add value – but they do. Without adding value, even though prices are low, the business will not be able to make a profit. Adding value is essential for all businesses and throughout your course you will find many examples of this.

Besides the need to maintain profitability, all businesses need to add value to remain competitive.

To remain competitive

The single European market gives businesses the right to sell their goods and services in any member state of the EU. In addition, increasing globalisation has led to businesses from across the globe selling in the UK. This globalisation also offers opportunities for British businesses, but they must remain competitive to succeed. The UK is very successful in many areas, such as software development, banking and other financial services.

Maintaining a leading position in these industries requires businesses to continue to add value to their products and outpace their competitors. Not all businesses have succeeded in this and more traditional British industries such as car production and coal mining have lost out to overseas rivals.

To meet customer requirements

Consumers are increasingly sophisticated and expect better services and higher quality products. If businesses are not able to meet the needs of customers, they will find it difficult to sell their products and services. As consumers' incomes rise, new products and services are required and businesses need to adapt to these changes.

Businesses can meet these needs by:
1 producing products consumers want
2 making sure the price is right
3 ensuring that the product/service is available in the right place at the right time
4 informing and persuading customers to buy their product or service.

In the 1960s many British businesses concentrated on manufacturing and did not sufficiently take account of the customer. These businesses were thought to be product oriented and very few of them have survived. Businesses increasingly recognise that they need to be market oriented to survive and their efforts need to go into meeting the needs of their actual and potential customers. This allows successful businesses to add value and charge a higher price; for example, Ben and Jerry's ice cream is sold as a high-class product. In a market-driven economy, the customer is king.

To survive and grow

Increasing added value is essential if businesses wish to expand and develop. Managers recognise that the only certainty in business is that change is inevitable; those organisations that cannot adapt will go out of business.

To please the shareholders

All businesses have to make adequate returns on their investment. Financiers, whether shareholders or friends, expect to see a return on their funds. Businesses need to meet their obligations or they will face stern criticism from their financial backers.

Quality control

In an increasingly competitive environment, consumers expect the best. They want high quality products and services, delivered at a time to suit them. Quality has always been important for the success of a business, but in today's competitive world it often means the difference between survival and closure. Businesses that cannot guarantee the quality of their products and services are unlikely to survive for long.

The focus of all quality initiatives must be the customer, whether in the public or private sector. Quality is not an end in itself, it is a means of providing excellence to the customers.

There is a large range of quality systems, each aiming to ensure goods and services meet the needs of consumers. Some of the well-known systems include:

- The government's Charter Mark
- The Investors in People Initiative
- ISO 9000
- British Standards Institute's Kitemark
- The Business Excellence Model.

ACTIVITY

Investigate one of the well-known quality systems to discover how it could affect a business.

Quality systems can be imposed by external agencies, but most organisations argue that quality is everyone's business and all staff have to be committed to improving the quality of everything they do. Businesses often use a quality assurance certification scheme like ISO 9000 to ensure it all happens. Whatever system is used, and all organisations need a system, its effectiveness is determined by how successfully it is implemented by all staff. Employees and managers will need to be trained and quality needs to be considered in all decisions. Most organisations have a training and development programme which aims to improve the effectiveness of the business.

The following systems have been used by various businesses to improve their quality.

TQM or Total Quality Management

This approach relies on all workers taking responsibility for achieving quality. It commits the organisation to continuous review and improvement of all activities relating to the quality of output and the satisfaction of customers. It is difficult to achieve as it often requires a change in an organisation's culture.

To be successful TQM needs to be led by senior management and those implementing it will need extraordinary patience and good communication skills.

Table 1.12 *The benefits of TQM*

Benefits	Difficulties
Improved quality	Ensuring senior managers' involvement
Increased productivity	Long time to implement and people become impatient for results
Businesses are more competitive	Bringing about the change in culture needed
Release of employee potential	Customer service may suffer as employees concentrate on improvements
A more motivated workforce	Those organising the project may lack vision, planning and leadership skills
Increased profits	
Reduction of waste due to zero defects	

Quality Circles

This approach began in Japan and is based on motivating employees by regularly involving them in business decisions. Small groups of workers meet regularly to discuss problems and find solutions. The approach uses the knowledge, experience and expertise of the workforce whilst making them feel a strong part of a team.

The system works best if employees volunteer, although it can still be a success if staff are co-opted. Employees will need training and development in methods of quality control, problem solving and communication skills. Vital ingredients for success include selecting the right group leader and for the management to consider carefully the recommendations and suggestions made by the various groups. If this doesn't happen, the groups feel they are wasting time sitting around talking through issues that no one takes any notice of.

This approach can lead to a change in attitudes and a reduction in conflict between team members. This, in itself, improves motivation and leads to increased output and quality of product/service.

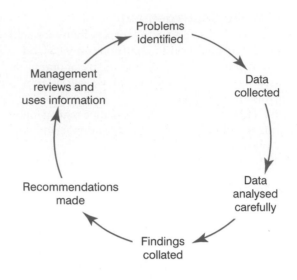

Figure 1.34 Quality circle

Self-assessment

Many organisations have been through quality processes such as those outlined above and have received the various kite marks, awards, and so on. They often feel the way forward is through continual self-improvement and assessment; for example, schools and colleges are inspected by OfSTED and then design their own self-assessment scheme. Similarly many small businesses use a self-assessment technique and often adopt a framework provided by their industry. The National Day Nurseries Association, for example, provides a quality assurance package based on the principle of monitoring performance against a set of criteria that define a high quality provider of day care for children. The main problem with this approach to quality assurance is that most organisations and individuals find it difficult to be self-critical and tend to view their work and performance through rose-tinted spectacles.

Benchmarking

Organisations using a self-assessment approach find it useful to compare themselves with similar organisations to see how they measure up. They compare key performance indicators using the same measures so that they can see whether their standards and performance are better or worse than those of their direct competitors. They are then able to pinpoint areas for improvement and will usually design an action plan to enable this to happen.

Want to know more?

Six sigma

'You really want zero but will you settle for six?' These are not the words of sales staff but of quality managers trying to deliver as close to zero defects as possible. Six sigma is, for now, the closest many can come.

What exactly is 'six sigma'? It was developed 12 years ago by the Motorola group for use in manufacturing. It is a measure of standard deviation and the higher the value, the fewer the problems for a company. It measures the quality of any manufactured product and records the number of defects per million (DPMs). For example, if a company's production line is achieving one sigma, it would signify there are 690,000 defects in every one million units. As a company performance improves, the value of sigma rises. So 45,000 DPMs would be recorded as two sigmas and the ultimate recording of six sigmas recognises there are only 3.4 DPMs, i.e. 99.99 per cent fault free.

There are very few one-sigma companies since that level of defects would quickly put any company out of business. Most manufacturers hover around four sigma or 6,000 DPMs. This might sound good but it isn't. Consider a mobile phone with 400 components: if the company operates at the two sigma level for each component, the chances are that virtually every phone will have something wrong with it.

General Electric has spent some $500 million on the first two years of its six-sigma venture. The Six Sigma Academy in Arizona estimates that the cost to companies of fixing defects at the four sigma level averages about 10 per cent of turnover.

So this is the end. How has it gone so far? Are there any things you've found difficult to understand? Why not go back over these now?

Appendix

Key Legislation

Companies Acts (1985 and 1989)

These Acts place responsibilities on companies, particularly regarding the way in which they prepare their published accounts.

COSHH – Control of Substances Hazardous to Health Regulations (1988)

The regulations require employers to identify hazardous substances in the workplace and control people's exposure to them (e.g. by careful handling, storage, and labelling, prompt clearance of spillage and provision of adequate ventilation).

Data Protection Acts (1984, 1998)

These Acts cover businesses, the self-employed and homeworkers who keep information, no matter how little, on computer about any living person. Almost any information other than a name, address and telephone number (with a few other exceptions) places an obligation to register with the Data Protection Registrar. Individuals have the right to see any computerised information held on them and to have incorrect information amended or deleted.

Once a business is registered, a Code of Practice is issued which requires the business to:

- keep the information secure
- ensure the information is accurate and relevant to its needs
- comply with individuals' right to see any computerised information held on them and to have incorrect information amended or deleted.

Electricity at Work Regulations (1989)

These regulations cover general safety in the use of electricity which includes the operation and maintenance of electrical equipment in a business. They provide for:

- regular checking of equipment by a competent person (not necessarily an electrician)
- listing of checks in a record book, stating results, recommendations, action taken in the case of defects and signature of the competent checker.

Employers Liability (Compulsory Insurance) Act (1969)

This Act places a duty on employers to take out and maintain approved insurance policies with authorised insurers against liability for bodily injury or disease sustained by employees in the course of their employment.

Factories Act (1961)

This places an obligation on an employer to provide a safe place of work.

Fire Precautions Act (1971) (updated in 1976)

The Act requires a business to provide fire-fighting equipment in good working order, readily available and suitable for the types of fire likely to occur. The Act also specifies that room contents should not obstruct exits, so that a quick escape, in the event of fire, is not impeded.

Gas Safety (Installation and Use) Regulations (1984)

This relates to the use and maintenance of gas appliances used in a business. British Gas and Health and Safety Executive inspectors have the right to enter premises and disconnect dangerous appliances under the Right of Entry Regulations (1983).

Health and Safety (First Aid) Regulations (1981)

The regulations stipulate that all businesses must have an appropriate level of first aid treatment available in the workplace. This means that businesses must:

- appoint a person to take charge in an emergency and look after first aid equipment. There must be an 'appointed person' available at all times during working hours.
- provide and maintain a first aid box containing information/guidance on the treatment of injured people
  - how to control bleeding
  - how to give artificial respiration
  - how to deal with unconsciousness
- display notices which state:
  - locations of first aid equipment
  - name of person(s) responsible for first aid.

Health and Safety at Work Act (1974) (updated by Workplace Health and Safety Welfare Regulations 1992 (EC Directives))

Employers should ensure the provision of adequate toilet and washing facilities, machines that are electrically safe, and protective clothing or equipment; they must ensure that precautions are taken when using chemicals; they must provide a clean and tidy workplace and workforce. The self-employed, home workers, and people who work alone away from employers' premises are included.

Employers are required to:

- provide systems of work that are, so far as is reasonably practicable, safe and without risk to health.

Employees have responsibility to:

- take reasonable care of themselves and other people affected by their work
- co-operate with their employers in the discharge of their legal obligations.

Offices, Shops and Railway Premises Act (1963)

The Act stipulates minimum standards to ensure a safe and healthy working environment. In conjunction with the Health and Safety at Work Act, it relates to every part of a business's premises.

Businesses should also make provision for a clean, tidy, well-lit, well-ventilated and well-maintained workplace, a clean and tidy workforce, adequate toilet and washing facilities, machines that are electrically safe, protective clothing or equipment, control of noise and vibration, accident and fire prevention, the safe use of chemicals and dangerous substances, and safe transportation and handling of materials.

Sunday Trading Act (1994)

If the floor area of the sales area is less than 280 square metres there are no restrictions on opening hours on Sunday; otherwise retailers can only open for six hours.

Index